DUTCH
In Sickness and in Health

DUTCH COURAGE
In Sickness and in Health

By Dirk van Zuylen

To Sally,

With every good wish,

Dirk van Zuylen

alpha

Copyright © 1999 Dirk van Zuylen

First Published in 1999 by Alpha

05 04 03 02 01 00 99   7 6 5 4 3 2 1

Alpha is an imprint of Paternoster Publishing,
PO Box 300, Carlisle, Cumbria, CA3 0QS, UK
http://www.paternoster-publishing.com

The right of Dirk van Zuylen to be identified as the Author of this
Work has been asserted by him in accordance with the Copyright,
Designs and Patents Act 1988

*All rights reserved. No part of this publication may be reproduced,
stored in a retrieval system, or transmitted in any form or by any
means, electronic, mechanical, photocopying, recording or otherwise,
without the prior permission of the publisher or a licence permitting
restricted copying. In the UK such licences are issued by the
Copyright Licensing Agency,
90 Tottenham Court Road, London W1P 9HE*

British Library Cataloguing in Publication Data
A catalogue record for this book is available from the British Library

ISBN 1-858938-68-7

Unless otherwise stated, Scripture quotations are taken from the
HOLY BIBLE, NEW INTERNATIONAL VERSION
Copyright © 1973, 1978, 1984 by the International Bible Society.
Used by permission of Hodder and Stoughton Limited. All rights reserved.
'NIV' is a registered trademark of the International Bible Society
UK trademark number 1448790

Cover Design by Mainstream, Lancaster
Typeset by WestKey Ltd, Falmouth, Cornwall
Printed in Great Britain by
Caladonian International Book Manufacturing Ltd, Glasgow

Contents

	Foreword	vii
1.	Childhood and Canada (1945–56)	1
2.	Teenager (1956–62)	9
3.	Holland (1962–67)	18
4.	England and Sandra (1967–68)	32
5.	Beirut (1968)	41
6.	Marriage and Family (1969–75)	52
7.	The Kidney Machine (1976)	65
8.	Life on Dialysis (1976–77)	81
9.	Sandra's Perspective (1979)	93
10.	Kidney Transplant (1979–80)	99
11.	A New Start in Manchester (1980–81)	112
12.	Holiday in America (1982)	125
13.	Pain and Pleasure (1982–88)	136
14.	Renal Failure Again (1989)	152
15.	Darkness (1990–92)	168
16.	The Second Transplant (1992)	190
17.	New Horizons (1994–98)	207

To three life-givers
Adriana, my mother
Sandra, my wife
Wilma, my sister

'One day I'm gonna write, the story of my life.'

Burt Bacharach wrote a song about it. My Dad wished he had written his.

Someone said to me 'Everyone has a *book* in them'. Few have the privilege of writing their story. It wasn't always an easy story to tell but I was glad to tell it.

'Without you I could never have written this story,' can be a bit of a cliché but it is certainly true of my mum, my wife and my sister.

I also want to acknowldege the debt due to Bob, Jean and Bill Croson. To Bob and Jean because they believed I had a story to tell before I did. To Bill because when he was seriously ill I didn't know what to say. This book is my guilt offering.

Thank you Bethan Ferguson for editing the first draft and Cathie Bartlam for your helpful suggestions.

I also want to thank . . . There are too many to name, I might miss one out. You know who you are.

Foreword

I don't like to see people suffering, I shy away from thinking about it. I usually turn the TV off, when the prying newsman's camera exposes the misery of suffering people, I could only read Dirk's book a chapter at a time, because it was too painful for me.

I not only read about Dirk's renal failure, I also witnessed it first hand. In 1976 as his kidneys began to fail, Mary, my wife and I were part of a group of Christians with Dirk, working with the Navigators in the North of England.

Like Job, we do not eaily discover why Dirk was put through those experiences, but we do learn how much he went through, and for how long, and I found it very disturbing.

Just as Job's counsellors brought him scant comfort, so some well-meaning Christians came to him with their verses and pat answers. As Job's troubles multiplied, so Dirk's ills increased as his life ebbed away, and even the ability to pray and enjoy people, characteristic of the man, was taken away from him.

The pain was not confined to Dirk only, Sandra, his wife bears the scars. Mark was hit with diabetes in the very year Dirk's kidney function totally failed and Mandy and Stephen suffered too.

How does Dirk see God's love expressed to him in his suffering? The surprising answer to me is — through people. I can see it also in the solace of his garden. [I have a dahlia that he gave us three years ago, luscious and beautiful it flowers again and again.] Then there are the Arts and the movies on video, that sustained Dirk in the long hours of dialysis.

After reading this simply written, moving and memorable account we may be able to see his God with greater awe.

James Fox

1

Childhood and Canada (1945–56)

'For unto us a child is born'
Handel's Messiah

'Did we ever tell you about the time Dirk was born?' my Dad would say, not waiting for an answer. We had heard the story a hundred times before. He would get up and walk around the room making a 'peep, peep,' sound acting as if he was looking for something. What was he looking for – a mouse? What he thought was a mouse was actually the weak cry of their newborn baby, not strong enough to make a more boisterous sound.

It was the last year of World War II, victory was in sight but a terrible winter held Holland in its grasp. Many people were dying of starvation. It was a bad time to be pregnant, with a baby expected in the middle of the winter. What if the child arrived at night? Could a doctor be found to deliver the baby?

So it was with some difficulty that my dad finally found one who would be willing to make the dangerous journey. People were often picked up off the street to be taken away to work camps in Nazi Germany and would never be heard of again.

In fact my dad had a pretty harrowing experience himself. He was cycling along on his bicycle (a bumpy ride as they had no tyres but only old rags wrapped around the wheels) when suddenly soldiers appeared, forcing people into vans. When they accosted my dad he explained to them that he was exempt because he had to look after his sick father and worked in the essential area of food production.

He was taken to an officer, his heart pounding. Some words were exchanged between the soldier and the officer that my father couldn't understand. Neither he nor the Germans could understand each other's language. Suddenly the officer bellowed something at my Dad, '*Fahr Auf*'. What did this mean? Go home? Get back into the line? He didn't know, he just picked up his bike and slowly rode off. If he had misunderstood the command he could have been shot. He heard more shouting but he did not dare to look back. He peddled away going faster and faster until he was out of sight, and could go no further. Riding his bike into the ditch he fell to the ground, weeping and shaking uncontrollably. What would his pregnant wife and young son have done if he had been taken? 'I have never experienced fear like that in my life,' he later recalled.

The doctor who had agreed to come insisted that he could not deliver the baby at night unless there was adequate heating and especially lighting. Where could they obtain oil for the primitive lamps during a time as deprived as this? There weren't even the basic necessities for most people. My Dad had heard that some growers who had large greenhouses were given a limited amount of oil for use in the winter. Perhaps he could get some. 'Yes, you can,' said the owner of the greenhouse, 'but how are you going to pay?' Potatoes were offered in exchange for the oil.

My father grew whatever he could to make a living and during the war tobacco could fetch good prices, if you weren't caught growing it! He had secretly grown some. His tobacco had been sold to buy the five bushels of potatoes exchanged for the precious five litres of oil which was worth the equivalent of about eight weeks' work.

After all that trouble I had the audacity to be born in the daytime. However, things were not well after the birth because I was born with a low body temperature and hence the weak mouse-like cry.

Again the doctor was called, 'He needs *moederwarmte*,' – mother's warmth – so I was kept close to my mother's bosom until I overcame the hypothermia. Not quite a return to the womb but the next best thing.

When my grandfather heard about the need for heat in our home he promptly got on his *bakfiets*, which is a tricycle that has a large carriage compartment at the front – and cycled out to his greenhouse. In the greenhouse was a lighted coal-burning stove. He wrapped some sacks and his coat around the hot stove picked it up and placed it on the *bakfiets* and brought the still warm stove to our house! There was heat enough in the house now, too bad for the crops in the greenhouse.

I eventually gained an adequate weight and temperature but the prognosis was that I would remain vulnerable all my life.

These were hard days for the Dutch people in the 'hunger winter' of 1945. My parents had my two-year-old brother, Peter, to feed as well. When they sat down for a meal there would usually be only three slices of bread, one for each person. My brother would gobble his up in the hope of more. My Dad would often give him his slice and had to resort to eating tulip bulbs which are in fact toxic causing eczema, but there was some nourishment in them. As the war continued his health deteriorated but thankfully the war ended in the spring of that year.

After this story was told it wasn't long before the next one was told in the usual style, as if it was being told for the first time. 'Did we ever tell you about the time your dad threatened to punch the doctor on the nose if they hurt Dirk again?' Groans were heard all around but undeterred the story was told.

As a lively two-year-old there's nothing quite like investigating your grandma's cupboard. Ah, a bottle – there's something left in it to try. The liquid was lye, a strong alkaline substance used to unblock drains. Immediately my mouth and throat began to swell up making breathing almost impossible. I was rushed to the hospital where a tube was forced down my throat to keep it open.

'It was very distressing for us,' said my mum. 'They had to strap your hands to the bed to keep you from pulling the tube out. Because of the tube you couldn't speak or even cry for that matter. As we sat by your bedside holding your little hand, the tears would roll silently down your cheeks.'

The tube needed to be changed from time to time using steadily larger ones to stretch the oesophagus. My mum couldn't face going to the hospital any more so my dad came on his own but I was very frightened. 'If they hurt you I'll give them such a punch in the nose that they'll never hurt you again.' This seemed to give me the assurance I was looking for.

Really getting into the swing of it now, and egged on by my children another story was told. 'Did we ever tell you about *Dirk de houthaler* – the wood carrier – or about the time Dirk told the farmer's wife that he had never had one of the eggs she had given us?'

When I was four our family emigrated to Canada. There were three of us now – my sister Mary had been born shortly before we left. Many Dutch people left to go to the 'New World' from post-war Europe. It was felt by many that the continent would never recover from the devastation of World War II. The US, Canada and Australia were seen as the lands of 'milk and honey'. A sponsor was needed however, and my Dad received a sponsorship from an apple farmer in Waterdown, Ontario. The farmer had built a wooden summer house for his children and this was to be our home. Not exactly ideal for the Canadian winters!

The move wasn't easy for my mum who had left her aging mother and all her brothers and sisters behind thinking she would never see them again. They had a cosy little house in Holland with their family and friends around them. All this was left behind for an unknown life in an unknown world, not even able to speak the language. What would have gone through her mind as she prepared the food on the pot-bellied stove in the kitchen of her two-roomed shack? The farmer had expected them to be homeless refugees and therefore grateful for anything. The house didn't even have internal doors, the kitchen was separated by a curtain from the lounge, where the five of us slept. There was no inside toilet which made for very cold treks outside in the winter.

But for a boy of four it was a place of high adventure especially because there was a war-surplus aeroplane on the farm which had been bought for spare parts for farm machinery. Peter and I had such fun imagining ourselves soaring through the skies in daring exploits.

My job was to bring the wood from the shed to the house. A pram with no wheels was used for this and I would drag it across the snow with great determination. 'Time for lunch,' my mother called! No reply was given, I wasn't going to come until I had finished the job. Thus I earned the name '*Dirk de houthaler*'.

My dad and I visited the farmer's mother who was a kindly old lady who supplied us with eggs free of charge. 'I never get an egg,' I said, looking innocent enough but telling a barefaced lie. She gave my father a look of disgust. 'Here's one especially for you, dear,' she said placing one gently into my outstretched hand. My father assured the nice lady that the eggs were shared amongst the whole family and that in no way was I neglected though she didn't seem convinced by his explanations. In fact, at Easter time, a Dutch custom was that we could have as many eggs as we could eat. I don't remember what was said to me after we got home but the incident impressed them enough to stay indelibly imprinted on their memory. Why do they need to keep reminding me?

After staying at Belvedere Orchards for a year we moved to Hamilton, a large steel-making city on Lake Ontario. We moved into a three-bedroomed house which was useful, as a new baby sister, Wilma, was soon to arrive. The house was located within the city limits but my dad's five-acre field was a few miles out. He specialised in growing cut flowers like gladioli, asters, zinnias and tulips. In the autumn, bulbs were sold at the local market and in the winter, Christmas wreaths were made and sold.

My jobs continued and now I became '*Dirk de waterhaler*'. This new name was acquired for carrying water to my dad as he worked in the hot summer sun, later to be changed to '*Dirk de potjeszetter*' for placing pots over the newly planted asters to keep them from shrivelling up in the heat.

The 'field' as we called it, was a wonderful place for making great road systems for the 'Dinky' toys. As I grew older there was more work to be done, so most of my free time was spent helping out in the field, hoeing, weeding and cutting flowers. However, when I was not working or at school I could be found out in the large wooded area nearby that had a stream running through it. School and I never really seemed to get on too well. My report card kept saying 'indifferent', though I didn't know what this word meant and just to prove the point, didn't try to find out the meaning! I preferred the great outdoors of Canada and my best pal Brian Taylor and I would often go 'back to the bush' as we called it to fish, walk or hunt. Catfish and perch were caught and sometimes cooked over an open fire. If we caught nothing there's nothing quite like eating sardines straight from the can sitting around the campfire and perhaps reading '*Field and Stream*'. We used to try to shoot birds with our B-B gun as well though I hope now that we didn't kill any! When we got bored with this we would take pot-shots at each other. Crazy, but 'boys will be boys'!

2

Teenager (1956–62)

'Lonely Boy'
Paul Anka

The fifties was a great time to be a teenager. We were creating a new identity for ourselves, separate from our parents. Television gave access to new role models in an unprecedented way. I'll never forget when Elvis appeared on television for the first time. Everyone at Westdale Secondary School, which I now attended, was talking about it. No one had ever sung, moved, or looked like this! The fact that our parents were outraged caused us to like him even more. Hair styles changed as quickly as we could get our hair to grow. The aim was to make a quiff that defied gravity but for this a little help from Brylcreem was needed: 'Brylcreem, a little dab'll do ya. Watch out the gals'll all pursue ya,' went the advertising jingle but what battles the length of my hair caused at home! A haircut at the local Italian barber's was not within the family budget, so my Dad cut mine with hands that were more used to clipping hedges. They didn't want their son looking like a juvenile delinquent. No chance of that with my pudding basin hairstyle!

Style of clothing changed considerably too. My favourite outfit to go dancing in was a gold and green shiny shirt, black tightly fitting jeans with red socks that had silver threads throughout. I had to save a long time to buy white buckskin shoes. I also managed to get hold of a black leather jacket that was covered with studs and had zips everywhere. My parents didn't seem to like it much and if I ever tried to hitch-hike somewhere I never got a lift!

Seeing James Dean in *Rebel Without a Cause* clarified things for us even more. He taught us how to smoke, slouch, put our collars up and especially to mumble when speaking to adults, with whom we had as little contact as possible.

Having 'necking parties' at your mate's cellar was great fun. Buddy Holly songs could be heard in the background as you played 'spin the bottle'. My brother and I collected every one of his records. When Buddy Holly appeared in Hamilton in concert at the ice rink we just had to go to see him even if it meant telling my parents a lie. Music was the teenagers' common language and gave expression to our feelings. 'Rock Around the Clock,' sang Bill Hailey. 'Only the Lonely,' lamented Roy Orbison. I wasn't allowed to have the radio on full volume so I used to listen with my ear right up against the speaker just able to make out the sound.

Some pictures that I had taken at one of our parties somehow found their way into the hands of my teacher. After looking through them with disgust she handed them back to me, scornfully referring to me as 'the rock and roll kid.' No greater honour could be paid to me!

When I was thirteen I used to wait for my pals at the school gate. On one occasion an attractive girl came up and asked if I was waiting for her. 'No,' I said the first and second time but by the third time even I knew this was an opportunity not to turn down from the sexiest girl in the class. I soon stopped collecting stamps and reading books. I stopped spending as much time as possible in Canada's great outdoors to begin the more exciting hobby of chasing girls. Once I got the hang of it I liked it better than any of my previous interests.

At that time photo booths began to spring up everywhere and many hours were spent trying to get that elusive shot that made you look like a 'rock star.' Some of the girls said I looked like Rick Nelson! They collected photographs of the boys they liked and some wrote song titles underneath. Under my picture one wrote 'Lonely Boy', a song written by a young Canadian teenager, Paul Anka.

When I was fifteen my brother and I bought a '54 Ford 'Meteor' and would go on double dates together, my brother, of course, having to drive with me in the back seat with my girl!! We were able to get home-made wine cheap from Italian immigrants. Less innocent pursuits followed and even though I didn't consider myself a bad youth I was very pleased when my role model brother said to me, 'You don't do many wild things but when you do they are really wild.' I remember coming home once not being able to walk very straight and my Dad asked me if I had been drinking. 'No,' I said looking him as straight in the eye as I could. His patience was a big factor in my wanting to change my ways, but please not just yet!

My time at high school brought little distinction except a prize I had won at junior high for reading the most books in the school in that year. Not being very interested in academic work and needing to help my father in the flower business I left at fifteen.

Growing flowers was not an easy occupation in Ontario. The winters were very severe, great for snow but not for tender flowers. To supplement the family income I took a job working for Cromwell Construction Company.

The alarm went off at 6:00 am. It was time to get ready for the one-hour drive to work. My usual sandwiches of Dutch cheese and bacon were ready, lovingly prepared by my mum. Off I set not realising what the day held, feeling only that it was far too early to be on the road. After arriving at work the first thing to look forward to was the arrival of the van which brought the coffee-break goodies like doughnuts, cookies and cake.

The firm I worked for specialised in pipe laying and this is what I was doing when something happened which was to subsequently change my life. I was working in a hole about ten foot deep, shored up with braces on either side to stop the walls from caving in. Joe, the bulldozer operator, was pushing soil to the edge of the trench with a view to back-filling it later when suddenly someone gave a shout. The bulldozer's front blade had accidentally got caught in the surface of the road and was pushing a huge slab of concrete into the trench. I ran like mad but as the slab thundered down it crushed my hand against the wall of the trench. I was rushed to the hospital where some particles of concrete were removed, skin grafts were carried out and the cut was stitched up. Thankfully the only lasting damage was an insignificant loss of feeling in my thumb.

It was a miraculous escape and a visit from the pastor drew my attention to this fact. 'Where would you have been if you had been killed?' he gently enquired. I had my response well prepared. My dad was an elder in the church so I had plenty of knowledge about the failings of these so-called Christians to deflect this awkward question.

Nevertheless he had shaken me up by drawing attention to my eternal destiny and I began to pray at night before I went to bed that I might one day become a Christian. From childhood I had been taught to pray:

'Here, Dank u dat gij mij deze dag bewaard heb. Geef mij vroeg en nieuw haartje.' 'Lord, thank you for keeping me this day. May I soon have a new heart.'

Every Sunday we went to what was called a 'gospel church' called Philpott Memorial in the city centre. Even though my parents were both from the Dutch

Reformed tradition they felt more at home in this church.

One of the characteristics of this church was an 'altar call' every Sunday night after a powerful sermon on the need for repentance.

> Just as I am, without one plea
> But that thy blood was shed for me,
> And that Thou bid'st me come to Thee,
> O Lamb of God, I come, I come.

So sang the choir. A further sense of drama was added by the painting at the front of the church. There was a large reproduction of Holman Hunt's *Light of the World* with these words underneath, 'Behold I stand at the door and knock'.

For many months I felt I heard that knocking and desperately wanted to go forward, but just couldn't in front of all those people, and especially my brother!

As time went by however, it got much easier to attend these services. If my eyes were open they were viewing the pretty girls, if they were closed I was enjoying a nice dream about pretty girls.

Nevertheless, I was disturbed that I was becoming more indifferent towards the Christian message. My thoughts about the afterlife were, that if I didn't want to live for God in this life, why should he take me to be with him in later life – but these thoughts scared me.

I decided I needed to do something about my situation so I asked if I could see the pastor. He was a burly Scot named Pastor Stien. We went up to his office and on the way up he said something that really scared me, 'You are going to leave this room a different person. You'll be a Christian or you'll become harder.'

I don't actually remember what we talked about but as he was speaking I had a very strange experience of feeling inwardly joyful. The feeling soon passed but I remember thinking, 'That's it, that's what I want, I want that joy.' Nevertheless when Pastor Stien asked if I wanted to let Jesus come into my life, I said, 'No, I'm too proud.' I wanted to run my own life.

'Let's pray,' he said and suddenly this big man got down on his knees. What could I do? I got down on my knees with him. The next thing I knew I was inviting Jesus into my life. 'Behold I stand at the door and knock' it said under Holman Hunt's painting. 'If anyone opens the door and invites me in, I will come in and eat with him,' went the rest of the quotation, and that's what I did. To this day I never felt as if I made a decision, it was as if God dragged me to the table to sit down with Jesus.

I went home in my '51 Pontiac singing away at the top of my voice with the windows open. I didn't care, I was saved!

I got into the bed I shared with my brother and told him what had happened. He received it with an obliging grunt. My parents were more forthcoming and expressed their delight. My mother later recalled that it was one of the happiest moments of her life.

Another rather useful temporal benefit of the accident was that I received compensation money until I was able to return to work. This was a great help in getting the family through the cold winter as there was very little opportunity for my dad to make enough money at this time.

Eventually after 14 years in Canada, my parents unexpectedly decided to return to Holland. At seventeen I felt that I was too young to stay in Canada on my own so Peter and I planned to go with them with the intention of returning after a year. It was very difficult for my mum who felt she might lose her sons because of this move. Even though my parents initially emigrated with the full intention of staying, the hard winters had taken their toll on my dad especially. He just couldn't take the prospect of another year of such hardship.

One incident which I think broke him more than any was the destruction of a partly built greenhouse by a freak storm. With great hope we were building a new larger greenhouse and only had one more side to finish. We had covered the vulnerable end with plastic sheeting but it was not able to withstand the ferocity of the typhoon. I'll never forget the tears as we together picked up the broken pieces scattered all over the hard ground.

It was difficult to make enough money in the summer for a family of seven to last through the barren winter. Sometimes help was given from the church, but the humiliation of receiving a basket of root vegetables was very hard to receive for a man who worked so long and hard to provide for his family, whatever the motive of the giver.

Because of the increased prosperity brought on by the Common Market and the possibility of accommodation, which was always a problem in overcrowded Holland, the opportunity was seized to go back.

Peter and I went across on the freighter *Poseidon* which was the cheapest way of crossing the Atlantic in the early winter of '62, leaving from Montreal. On board with us was his newly acquired red '56 Chevrolet, too important to him to be left behind. We received some special treatment, eating daily at the captain's table, that is if we weren't too seasick to enjoy the meal. My parents, together with Mary and Wilma and five-year-old brother John, had flown across earlier.

3

Holland (1962–67)

'What a friend we have in Jesus'

We arrived in Rotterdam, one of the largest ports in the world. My parents were there to pick us up and they drove us back through the Dutch landscape. Everything looked so different from what we were used to in Canada. The houses were very picturesque with their sloping tiled roofs and windows with pretty lace curtains that allowed a clear view into rooms full of plants and ornaments. Windmills stood beside canals that were all so straight and well maintained. Now and then we saw herons at the water's edge waiting for lunch to turn up.

Most things were on a smaller scale than we were used to with houses and farms built close together but the biggest impact was the number of people! I was told that Holland was one of the most densely populated countries in the world – though I could have deduced that just from looking around. I had never seen so many bicycles in my life and so many mopeds

Holland (1962–67)

too, which they called '*brommers*'. These machines buzzed around like angry bees. Thankfully there were specially laid out paths for these two-wheelers.

The perfectly laid out farms that usually had the farm buildings directly attached to the house were new to me. How do they cope with such proximity to the black-and-white cows which provide Holland with an over-abundance of manure, the secret of its agricultural success? The cows in Holland may look the same as the British Friesians but they do speak a different language. Cows in Britain say 'moo' but Dutch cows say '*boo*'. As we neared where we were to live, we were amazed to see greenhouses covering acres of land. We passed through the beautiful city of Leiden with its ancient university, classical Dutch buildings with the many-windowed frontage, and on to Rijnsburg where I was to live for the next four years. We lived in a typically Dutch semi built with tiny bricks. It had a low, sloping tiled roof. There were three bedrooms upstairs, but to call where my brother and I slept a bedroom might be too generous a description. We shared a double bed in what was really a loft space. One of my abiding memories of that first year was lying under a mountain of bed clothing watching my breath rise as my awakening eyes focused on frost-covered nails protruding from the ceiling.

One of the first things Peter and I needed to do was learn the language. We had tried to practise our Dutch on the way over to Holland but this usually ended up in raucous laughter as we struggled with the rolling '*r*' and the '*g*' sound which is made by clearing your throat. Quite handy if you have a cold! It all sounded like Double-Dutch to us. Someone said, rather disparagingly, that Dutch is more of a throat disease than a language. In fact most of the English references to the Dutch are derogatory, for example, 'Dutch treat' and 'Dutch courage'. These expressions were coined during periods of conflict with Holland in previous centuries.

At home in Canada we had usually spoken a mixture of Dutch and English. My parents would often address us in their native tongue and we would reply in ours. For some reason we always used the Dutch word *hempie* for undershirt and *onderbroek* for underpants.

Rijnsburg, which had recently celebrated its first millennium was a village of seven thousand inhabitants, most of whom were involved in growing or selling flowers. Central to the life of the village is the *veiling*. This is a huge covered market in which flowers are sold by 'Dutch auction'. Rather than the prices going up and being sold to the highest bidder, a big clock spins around, running down from the higher figure and the first person to press the button gets them at that price. He would then shout out how many bunches he wanted and around the clock would go again. My uncle who was considered to be a mathematical wizard did all the calculations in his head. He was eventually replaced by a computer! The *veiling* opened at 6:00 am so we had to have the flowers ready at that time which meant getting up very early. We would usually have to get up at 4:00 am to go to the greenhouses to pick and bunch the tulips so that they would be fresh and ready on time.

My dad had a very gentle way of waking us up. He would come upstairs, call us, give us a little nudge and say that breakfast was ready. He often needed to do this many times. The breakfast consisted of tea usually taken without milk and *biscuit*, a Dutch crispbake. After the flowers had been picked and taken to the *veiling* we would come back home for another breakfast which my mother would have prepared. Fresh hot Douwe Egberts coffee with its wonderful aroma awaited us as we sat down to discuss what prices we might get today. We were then off to the field again which incidentally was called the *galg*, which means 'gallows' for reasons I didn't want to find out! The most interesting time was when the growers got together at the coffee break and discussed all sort of things. They passed on growing tips, moaned about the prices of flowers, discussed people in the village – but especially they talked about the war. Having been an occupied country for the duration of the war gave them much to talk about. It was through these times that I realised how deeply the Dutch psyche had been affected by the war.

Our first winter in Holland was one of the coldest in living memory, the canals, lakes and even part of the sea froze over. Having left my excellent hockey skates behind in Canada thinking I would never need them again I found it quite a novelty to skate with wooden strap-on skates which were last seen in a Bruegel winterscape.

I didn't know many people at the time so my life seemed to revolve around working in the field during the day and reading books sitting around the coal-fired stove in the evening. I tackled *The Rise and Fall of the Third Reich*, Winston Churchill's four-volume *A History of the English-Speaking Peoples*, which I really enjoyed. Salinger's *The Catcher in the Rye* impressed me. *Dog of Flanders*, a tale of the heroic exploits of a dog in World War I made me cry. I also took out a subscription to *Time* magazine which I pretty well read from cover to cover.

Trips were made to the art galleries in Amsterdam. Perhaps I wasn't ready for van Gogh yet but I found Rembrandt and Vermeer fascinating. I bought my first reproduction at the Rijksmuseum. It was Rembrandt's painting of *Jeremiah Lamenting the Destruction of Jerusalem*. It is still hanging up in my office today as I write. I am charmed by the shaft of light pointing to the sad prophet. In later years the words of this man's lament impressed me deeply. I found a man who had trodden the path of darkness I was to tread, a kindred spirit and a role model.

I gradually started relating to my parents as an adult, having got over my teenage rebellion. Mine was probably quieter then my brothers though some would say sneakier.

My dad has a very active mind and is very serious about the issues of life, thinking deeply about many things. One of my dad's greatest strengths is his boundless determination to press ahead no matter what the obstacles. If one crop failed he would optimistically make plans for the next. In seeking to provide for his family he never gives up. There is a very tender and sensitive side to him as well. Home was a place of many lively discussions, sometimes getting quite heated, often about religion. The Bible was very central to our family life. Three times a day it was read at mealtimes along with prayer before and after every meal.

Sunday services at church were usually followed by lengthy discussions about the minister's sermon, with generous amounts of strong coffee to lubricate the proceedings. Sometimes fresh cream cakes were served too. Puffing away on a Dutch cigar completed the scene, giving a certain gravitas to the situation. There is a saying I heard at the time: 'One Dutchman – a theologian, two Dutchmen – a church, three Dutchmen – a new church'. Dutch church culture placed great value on theological correctness.

During the week I went to a young people's group where more discussions were held. I gradually learned that having an opinion and being able to express it clearly was very important in Holland.

My mum often took the peacemaker role in the family. Sometimes when affirmation was forgotten in the heated exchanges, she would reassure us of my father's love and tenderheartedness. She is a real 'lady', my mum, a woman of wisdom and grace. She is not tall but carries herself with dignity and dresses with real flair. She too is totally devoted to her family and seems to find joy in the service she gives to all. I have never heard her complain that anything we asked was too much trouble.

My new-found faith was making a great deal of difference to my life. I found a love in my heart that certainly wasn't there before. One of the first changes I noticed was that I was more tolerant and accepting of people I usually wouldn't have associated with, like students for example. I remember saying to one new friend called Dio that he was the first intellectual that I liked. His response was, 'You are the first dumb person I have ever liked!'

I did however find it particularly difficult to be loving at home. I was often bad-tempered and withdrawn. Sometimes I felt as if I had left my Christianity outside the door. I felt as if I was overtaken by some 'crabby bear' when I walked in the door. Mary, Wilma or John were often at the receiving end of my surliness.

I started attending an evangelical youth group in our village after numerous invitations by the coalman. He was a simple man with Pentecostal zeal who I found a bit embarrassing but he did eventually persuade me to go along to the group.

We used to sing a lot which I liked very much. One of my favourites was:

> What a friend we have in Jesus
> All our sins and grief to bear!
> What a privilege to carry
> Everything to God in prayer!

Preaching on street corners was however more challenging than singing! One of our more presumptuous escapades saw us preaching to churchgoers as they emerged from the morning service. Not many people listened to us, but we used to persuade ourselves that people were listening behind closed doors. When my turn came someone whispered in my ear just as I was about to start, 'Say you used to live in Canada,' as if my strong accent wouldn't have made that quite clear. The reason he said this was that Canadians were particularly popular because they had liberated Holland during the war. 'I used to live in Canada,' I said and then dried up completely. I couldn't think of anything else to say, my mind went completely blank. After a few catcalls I eventually regained my composure and continued, though I have no idea what I said after that.

We used to travel to meetings in a big furniture van. We sat on wooden benches placed on either side of the van, which meant that we arrived in a somewhat dishevelled state having been thrown around in the darkness.

It was at one of these meetings that I first came across the Navigators — an American-based group which specialised in helping young believers to get firmly grounded in their faith. They acquired this name because they originally were involved with American sailors whom they 'navigated' through the Christian faith. This was usually done on a one-to-one basis but from time to time teaching seminars were held which gave opportunity for talks from the Bible and small discussion groups.

The founder of the Navigators was a man called Dawson Trotman. He had been working with American sailors before the Second World War, teaching them by word and example how to live the Christian life. Before long a young sailor found a new Christian who was keen to learn and brought him to Dawson. 'Will you teach him what you taught me,' he asked. 'No,' Dawson replied 'You teach him what I taught you.' This was really the beginning of the movement! The ethos of the Navigators was to bring someone up in the faith until he is able to pass it on to another.

At that time my Dutch was still quite poor so I asked to be placed in an English-speaking group led by a newly arrived American called Lee Brase. He was a kind and gentle man with a friendly, unassuming manner. He was on the staff of the Navigators and had been trained by them to teach younger believers, primarily on a one-to-one basis.

I was challenged at the meeting to get to know my Bible better, and Lee offered to help. He gave me a study leaflet on the gospel of John. 'Fill this in,' he said, 'and return it to me for marking. I'll then send you the next leaflet.' The question-and-answer study was duly filled in and sent to Lee who returned it with some helpful comments made in red pencil. This rather quaint way of doing things was the beginning of a lifelong friendship.

Lee was a frequent visitor to our home in Rijnsburg and I think my parents were quite pleased that I listened to him. He could point out things in

Holland (1962–67)

my life that my parents wouldn't dare to. One day my dad and I were having a long-drawn-out discussion about the best route to Amsterdam, in which I insisted that my way was the quickest. Afterwards Lee said to me, 'Do you think it really would have made much difference?' 'Well, er . . . no, I guess.' I had to acknowledge that he had a point. He used to say to me, 'It's not what you say, it's the way you say it.'

When a friend of mine became a believer he asked me how I was going to help him. As the thought had never occurred to me, I said that I had no idea what to do. We sat down in his office with Lee sitting on one side of the desk and me on the other. He proceeded to give me a little sermon on how to help a new Christian while I took notes.

We did lots of things together. When he had visitors from America he would often invite me to join them as we visited the tourist sights of Holland, like the miniature village of Maduradam, for example. It gave me a chance to see a bit of my home country!

I would visit him where he and his wife Marilyn, who was a lively counterpart to his more quiet nature, would always make me feel at home. Often we would spend time having lively discussions around an open Bible. Praying together united our hearts.

They invited me to join their family now living in Amsterdam. This was an opportunity to team together to take the Christian message to students and other young people in this fascinating city.

I continued to help my father, working with him two days a week. (It wasn't easy for the family because it meant that Mary and Wilma had to do a lot more work in the fields.) I had to make the hour-long journey back and forth to Amsterdam by *brommer*, twice a week. During the winter I would arrive feeling like a block of ice after the trek along the poplar tree-lined roads through the cold wet *polders*.

Along with Lee and Marilyn and their two-year-old daughter Amy, were two other young men called Dio and Frake. A young women called Gratia was also there to help in the busy home. We were one big happy family. Well, for most of the time that was!

Another reason for living with the Brases was to receive help in my Christian life. Part of this had to do with character training. I was quite keen on this idea at first until something happened that I didn't like! I was helping to set the table and as I reached into the cupboard to get some glasses I accidentally sent the whole row flying. They all went crashing to the floor. Lee accepted my apology graciously but suggested that if I concentrated more on what I was doing it might not have happened. I was incensed at first but had to acknowledge that he had a point. It wasn't the last careless thing we did either.

Lee and Marilyn had spoken from time to time about the desire to lay a carpet in our bedroom. The three of us decided we would give them a nice surprise and carpet the room while they were away one weekend. We presented them with our 'labour of love' when they returned only to find them less than enthusiastic about our handiwork. It transpired that our house being a rented one, permission was needed from the landlord to lay a carpet. We also learned that if he had given permission he may have preferred us to take up the linoleum floor first. This way it wouldn't have been full of holes made by our tacks!

When we weren't knocking over glasses or tacking carpets onto linoleum floors we did spend many hours studying the Bible, praying and discussing the things we were learning. I am very grateful for the good foundation this laid in my life. We also spent much time visiting the halls of residence to talk to students about Jesus.

Around this time Amsterdam was becoming a major attraction to young people from all over the world and especially the US. The city seemed to be teeming with colourful hippies looking for 'happenings'. The city has a long history of tolerance so this was the place to be to 'do your own thing' whether that was free sex or smoking marijuana. If you needed a place to stay you could sleep with your friend in the Vondel Park or break into a derelict building because squatter's rights assured you of secure accommodation. Many hung out at the Damrak square during the day.

The hippies even organised themselves into a political party called the *Provos* who won some seats on the city council. One of their plans was to make all bicycles public property. The reason the plan was never passed in council was probably because people were treating bikes as public property anyway! The simple locks were easily forced open, the bicycle ridden to wherever someone wanted to go and dumped. You were lucky if it wasn't chucked in the canal. Always a useful place for throwing unwanted goods as any visit to Amsterdam will show you.

It was while I was staying with the Brases that I was asked by another Navigator, Gene Soderberg, if I would like to join him in England for three weeks where he was training counsellors for the forthcoming visit of Billy Graham in 1967. It sounded like an opportunity that was too good to miss. I had always wanted to visit England and was very keen to help with the training of counsellors.

I travelled across country by train to Bradford. On the journey I fancied something to drink. The steward came over and said, 'Wot'll-it-be-me-duck.' I thought English was my first language but now I wasn't so sure. Anyway I asked for coffee to which the reply came, 'Black or white.' Black coffee I was familiar with but white? I had seen brownish coffee which I called 'coffee with milk or cream'. Eventually I realised what she meant and asked for 'white'.

Finally I arrived at the Victorian station in Bradford after my first course in Yorkshire English to be welcomed by Pastor Evans with whom I was to stay. He awakened me the next morning with a lovely cup of tea served in the British way with milk. This was a first for me. Another first was hearing someone being called 'luv' who wasn't a close relation. In Canada this term of endearment was reserved for only the most intimate of relationships. I was shocked!

He also introduced me to the Yorkshire Dales which I fell in love with at first sight. The green hills, the dry-stone walling, the churches nestling in picturesque valleys was something I had never seen the like of before. Visiting Fountains Abbey in the tranquil setting of its gardens was awe inspiring. Durham Cathedral was, and still is, my favourite cathedral because of its grandeur and strength. We stayed at various homes in the northern part of England and it was at a jeweller's home in Newcastle that I first saw Wedgewood pottery. I just had to take some back to Holland.

A special treat was coming back to the house and having supper, something that was quite new to me. Fish and chips served fresh and eaten out of a newspaper. Wonderful!

In the summer of that year I also spent two weeks in Cambridge which sealed my love of England. I left with an invitation to return in the autumn. I couldn't wait!

4

England and Sandra (1967–68)

'Leaving on a Jet Plane'
Peter, Paul and Mary

Something was clearly going wrong. I had dedicated my life to God and was serving him with single-minded devotion. I had decided that when I was twenty-five I might look into the possibility of finding a wife but not before, and now here I was only twenty-two and madly in love. This I had not reckoned on!

On my recent visit to England, Robb Powrie-Smith, who was responsible for the Navigator student group in Loughborough, had invited me to come back to join them as soon as I could. I was very keen to return because I had met some of the students and was very fond of them. Robb had asked me to establish these new Christians in the faith. In September 1967 I said goodbye to my family and friends in Holland and my father drove me to the Hook of Holland where I boarded the ferry bound for England.

England and Sandra (1967–68)

The ship arrived in Harwich very early in the morning and I was awakened by the sound of the cleaners going about the ship doing their work. I stumbled into the daylight and onto a deserted dockside, all the other passengers having disembarked long ago, to find a sign instructing me to go to the reception area where a message awaited me.

On presenting myself at reception they were not too keen to let me into the country. The immigration officials seemed to think that twelve shillings and sixpence was not enough money to enter the country with! After a phone call to my host Robb they reluctantly let me in. Off to Loughborough in the Midlands I went, hitch-hiking of course.

The family I came to stay with was a lively household to say the least. Students were always popping in for a chat or some food and there were seven of us resident. Robb and Meg Powrie-Smith with their two lively toddlers, Alistair and Anne, a student Bob Croson (who was to become a life-long friend), myself and Sandra who had left a good job as a lab-technician in Manchester to come and help in the family. Robb was a dynamic business man of Scottish origin and Meg had been a teacher. Both of them had left good jobs believing that God had called them to Loughborough to work with students.

The purpose of our being together was to create a welcoming 'home away from home' atmosphere for the students. In this context we would spend much time with them individually talking about their relationship to God, their family lives, their witness for Christ, their devotional lives, in fact anything they wanted to talk about. We would also get together on a weekly basis to study the Bible and listen to practical talks about the Christian life. It was a very life-on-life involvement. It was also an opportunity for me to receive tutoring in how to help people grow in their Christian lives. There was the added bonus of seeing family life close up which was to prove very useful later when I myself would have a family – but that thought was very far from my mind, at first anyway!

Sandra made an immediate impression on me by the way she so generously and sacrificially gave herself to people. I liked her spirit too and her sense of fun. When Bob, Sandra and myself were together there was always some fun being planned or executed.

At first I was too busy to notice, but little by little she was creeping into my thoughts. I didn't know how to handle this. Well it's mind over matter! You just block these things out of your mind. I had had other distractions before, 'I can handle this!'

This, however, was not as easy as I thought and I got myself into quite a confused state. When helping to clear the table somehow the things that were meant for the fridge found their way into the oven! 'Anyone can make a mistake can't they?' Jokes that were usually taken in good spirit suddenly caused strong reactions. Sandra too seemed to be more keen to serve me then the rest of the family. If I said that I liked something, like blueberry jam for example, there it would be on the table at the

England and Sandra (1967–68)

next meal, much to the chagrin of Robb, who never got that kind of preferential treatment.

I even took to singing 'Country and Western' songs to Sandra out of the bathroom window when she was out in the wash-house:

> The woman one day she was washing,
> the hot soapy water was sploshing.
> She tripped o'er the pot, and in it she sot
> and it got her behind in her washing.

'What's wrong with Dirk,' everyone was asking? 'Oh, he's a bit tired, what he needs is an early night.' Four strong students carried me off to bed.

Well, what does y'r average committed disciple do when he gets an early night? He reads his Bible of course, but 'Song of Solomon'? A love poem?

As I was reading I came across: 'Many waters cannot quench love, neither can the floods drown it'.

This was it. I knew I could fight it no longer. I had to admit that I was madly in love. But what should I do? 'Let's try to get to know her a little bit better, talk to her, spend some time together.'

Rather conveniently, a few days later, it so happened that it was just the two of us who were in for the evening meal. Sandra had made a lovely meal of savoury pancakes and there we sat looking at each other across the table feeling very self-conscious. One of the standard questions Christians ask one another when they are getting acquainted is, 'How did you become a Christian?' I tried that one. This didn't seem to get us very much further, so I tried a few more questions from the 'getting to know you' textbook. Nothing seemed to be working. 'There is no hope for this relationship if I can't even talk to her,' I thought, 'it really isn't working.'

What I didn't realise was that she was in fact quite interested in me and fear had suppressed her usual easygoing manner.

But on the whole, we did have a lot of fun together in those days, giving each other a lot of attention and pretending not to. I had played a trick on Sandra by writing some cheeky comments under a picture of her parents and she retaliated by dowsing my bed with her perfume, called 'Midnight'. I didn't know how to take this but Sandra maintains to this day that it was a perfectly innocent gesture. 'You said you liked my perfume,' she said, which indeed I did. Robb and I used to pray together in Sandra's bedroom which had a picture of some hunk on the wall. I took it down and put up a picture of myself instead with the caption 'this is a real man', written underneath. 'You will never see that picture again,' Robb said. I didn't understand what he meant but I did notice that the picture was taken down but not returned.

I was very much in love but frightened to tell her how I felt.

Playing games, pretending, but not really talking created quite a bit of internal turmoil. The tension in the home became unbearable so Robb felt he needed to break the deadlock. He and Meg were being plagued by two lovesick people keeping them up

England and Sandra (1967–68)

most nights with their fears of unrequited love, 'Will he ever love me?' or 'Will she ever love me?'

We were on our way from Cambridge having visited some friends there and I was saying to Robb how difficult it must be for Meg when he was away. 'Yes,' he replied, 'and it's pretty difficult for someone else when we're away as well.' 'Who?' I asked, not daring to guess. 'Sandra?' I couldn't believe it. 'You need to talk to her,' Robb replied. He phoned home and told Meg to keep Sandra up. Robb was a pretty fast driver but I told him if he didn't get a move on I'd have to get out and run!

Sandra was there waiting for me. She looked terrified! Robb and Meg suddenly disappeared and I ushered Sandra into the lounge. I sat her down, took hold of her hand and said, 'I love you, will you pray about marrying me?'

'Yes, I will,' she said, 'I've already prayed about it!'

We spent the rest of the evening and well into the early morning telling each other about our love for one another, only being interrupted by Robb and Meg from time to time to give reports on the proceedings.

The next morning I was talking with Robb in the bathroom, sitting on the edge of the bath, and fell in. He realised that I wouldn't be much use at work that day so we were given the day off. We borrowed Bob's car and off we set into the beautiful English Peak District. We went for blissful walks, hand in hand. There was so much to talk about.

We wanted to do something really special so we decided to go for a meal in a posh restaurant, not something we could really afford. The restaurant was nearly empty, the waiters looked like members of the Addams family and the food was awful, but we didn't care. We just giggled like children, or should I say like two people in love. We were together and nothing else mattered.

We had to cope with a lot of leg-pulling from our friends, though not everyone was equally pleased. Because Sandra had just broken off an engagement a couple of months earlier some felt the need to warn her about the need for caution. Someone else warned me about the need to not get distracted from my work and to 'get on with the job.' Another warned Sandra about the potential difficulties of getting involved with someone from another culture.

We hoped to be able to get married within a year so we arranged for me to go up to meet Sandra's parents in Manchester and for me to ask her father for Sandra's hand (and the rest of her too for that matter). Sandra's father delivered cakes for Bennett's Bakery and Sandra's mum worked in Mr Hill's cheese shop in Altrincham. She was a friendly, quick-witted person who was very welcoming to me. Sandra had spoken to her Mum about her love for me. 'It's all right for you to love him,' her mum said, 'but he's got to love you too.' I think she was assured on this point!

Sandra's parents were Lancashire people born and bred, and I was really taken by the Northern hospitality and easygoing manner. Sandra's father, from whom she seemed to inherit her easygoing, likeable nature, was a truly good man. Although he had suffered much as a prisoner of war there was no bitterness in him and he communicated acceptance to everyone he met.

The next morning Sandra asked me what her father had said. 'Said about what?' I enquired. 'About our getting married,' she replied. I had totally forgotten. Frantic phone calls to her dad at work elicited the necessary approval. This was very gracious of him seeing as I had no visible means of support and they hardly knew me.

Folk music was very popular at the time amongst students and especially 'Peter, Paul and Mary'. We had a very gifted group of musicians amongst the students, who loved to sing their songs. One that was very popular at the time was a John Denver song called 'Leaving on a Jet Plane'.

> All my bags are packed, I'm ready to go.
> I'm standing here outside your door,
> I hate to wake you up to say goodbye
> But the dawn is breaking, it's early morn.
> The taxi's waiting, blowing his horn,
> Already I'm so lonesome I could die.
>> So kiss me and smile for me,
>> Tell me that you'll wait for me.
>> Hold me like you'll never let me go.
>> I'm leaving on a jet plane
>> Don't know when I'll be back again.
>> Oh, babe, I hate to go.

> There's so many times I let you down,
> So many times I played around,
> But I tell you now, they don't mean a thing.
> Every place I go I, I'll think of you,
> Every song I sing, I'll sing for you.
> When I come back I'll bring your wedding ring.

We used to sing along to this song little realising that it would be a little more meaningful than we would have liked. One month later I would indeed be leaving on a jet plane, not knowing when I would be back again but comforted by the fact that when I came back I would indeed bring Sandra's wedding ring. I had been asked if I would be willing to go to Beirut to help out in a similar way as I had been doing in Britain. I certainly didn't feel like leaving the one I loved but I felt it was what I should do.

5

Beirut (1968)

'The Emperor'
Beethoven

'I'm sorry sir, but you have missed your connection to Beirut so you will have to stay in Rome compliments of Air Italia until tomorrow. We will, of course, arrange for you to stay in one of our best hotels.'

So said the man at the reception desk. 'Oh dear, I think I can cope with that!'

A day to explore Rome. This ancient city whose power and influence had extended throughout most of Europe and well into Asia. The buildings were so grand and the city so full of life. It was home to a church whose power extended over the whole world. Walking around a city that was the power base of such influence in culture, arts and religion was an amazing experience. Back at the hotel I felt truly important if a little self-conscious, as I sat enjoying the excellent food that the Italians are so justly famous for the world over. I hope I didn't look too out of place amongst all the high-powered business people. I felt like David in a room full of Goliaths!

The next day the flight took off for Lebanon with a stopover in Athens. We were given a few hours to look around. I especially liked the Grecian pottery with its graceful artistry and was compelled to buy some to take home with me. Contact with the two seminal cultures of Europe was a never-to-be-forgotten experience. Another ancient culture awaited me however, which was to have an even deeper impact on my life.

As we descended towards the airport we flew over the beautiful city of Beirut with its majestic mountains on the east and the palm-lined beaches on the west. It was quite breathtaking. Lebanon is sometimes called the Switzerland of the Middle East, because of its beautiful mountains and valleys and thriving economy. Its great history goes back to Phoenician times – some say that this seafaring race was the first to cross the Atlantic many years before Christ.

Nate Mirza, the Navigator leader in Lebanon, greeted me warmly at the terminal. I was to stay with him, his wife Kay and their two delightful little girls during my six-month stay.

We passed the ramshackle Palestinian refugee camps, that were to play such a major role in the coming years. I arrived a little under a year after the 'Six-Day War' of 1967 so the city was still unscarred because the fighting had been in south Lebanon. 'How are the Israelis going to take Lebanon?' 'By phone!' was a joke the Lebanese told at that time. I don't suppose anyone knew just how fierce the fighting would become. Having said that, the brooding violence of the taxi drivers in Beirut might have given them a clue!

Driving through the city in one of the hundreds of taxis called *service*, usually a fifties Mercedes, has to be experienced to be believed. They are totally a law unto themselves. Traffic inches its way forward under a great cacophony of horns and shouting and the shaking of fists. Radios blast out the rhythmic, passionate Arabic music. At junctions the right of way is taken by the first person into that junction. First come, first served! In Lebanon, if you drive into the side of someone who got there first, you are at fault even if the accident is caused by the negligence of the other driver.

I was to stay initially at a small family-run hotel just around the corner from the Mirzas. I was so excited to be in Lebanon. The next morning I was awoken by the wailing of the Muslim call to prayer, good enough for a Christian to rise to prayer too! After prayers the breakfast of freshly baked Arabic bread served with *labneh*, a concentrated yoghurt to which foreigners add jam, something the locals abhor. Strong Turkish coffee, half coffee, half sludge, in tiny cups, was served with this. Different to what I was used to but delicious.

A newspaper belongs with breakfast and fortunately there was an English-language paper published in Beirut. I soon noticed however that though the language was the same, the viewpoint was very different. One of the very significant differences was the way in which news items were presented on the Arab-Israeli conflict. In the West the Arabs are presented as launching unprovoked attacks on innocent Israelis. I remember during the Six-Day War thinking it was somehow a reliving of the heroic battles of Biblical times, identifying God as being on Israel's side. Reading newspapers here however gave a very different perspective. I read of Israeli atrocities and Lebanon defending its sovereignty in the south of the country. I had to acknowledge that my view of the conflict was much too simplistic and one-sided.

I loved the people I was beginning to get to know. They had such spirit and were so outgoing and friendly. I spent many hours with the students at the American University of Beirut talking about religion and politics. Not an unsuitable topic of conversation in polite company there. Talking to Palestinian students who had had to leave their homeland was illuminating. The strength of their passion they felt for their state was something I had never experienced before. Once when talking to someone about eternity, he said, 'I'd go to hell for Palestine,' and I knew he meant it.

I sometimes felt vulnerable walking the streets because Dutch people were not so popular with the Lebanese. Holland had given Israel support during the war and there was still strong feeling about this. I remember trying to get into Syria for a visit on the understanding that a visa would be available at the border. 'They shouldn't let a Dutchman in, with or without a visa,' the border guard said. I was summarily dismissed.

Beirut (1968)

I had been invited to go to Lebanon to help out on a temporary basis while two of the three missionaries were on furlough. One of my jobs was collecting items for a prayer calendar from the Navigator student leaders. On each day of the month there would be a different prayer request. These items needed to be sent to me for correlation by the 15th day of the month, but they never arrived on time. It was always *boukra*, tomorrow. I therefore had to go around to all the different people to collect the requests. I was irritated by this and said to one of them, 'I waste hours getting this information which I wouldn't need to if you responded on time.' This experience gave me incentive in the years to come to try to get my own work in on time. However, one of the reasons they didn't get the work to me on time was because they were more interested in spending time with people. As time went by I began to understand and appreciate their mindset.

Another formative experience happened at a party. Someone accidentally knocked over a drink. Expecting someone else nearby to clean it up I stood at a distance not particularly watching. After a while noticing that no one had done so, I went into the kitchen, got a cloth and began to clean it up. Some one eventually gave me a hand though he seemed quite embarrassed. I was perplexed by the fact that some Arabs seemed so reluctant to do menial tasks. In fact I felt quite judgemental towards them.

At the Mirzas' where I was now staying, I used to do a lot of practical jobs around the house and helped with the children. I even learned how to change a nappy! Once, when I was doing this, one of the Arab students came around and I quickly wheeled the baby into the bedroom so that he wouldn't see me doing this. He may have found it harder to respect me if he had seen me doing menial tasks. Later I had an experience that taught me that I wasn't so keen to do certain 'menial' tasks either.

I used to babysit sometimes for Nate and Kay and I remember Debbie being particularly fractious one night. The only thing that seemed to help was walking around carrying her against my shoulder. I thought to myself, 'Well, here you are "missionary", walking around with a baby when you are supposed to be out there preaching the gospel.' Suddenly it struck me. If I was babysitting for Joseph and Mary wouldn't I be only too pleased to walk around with Jesus if he was restless! I realised for the first time that serving a child is serving Jesus. What a privilege!

I was learning a lot about serving but after my initial love for all things 'Arab' it all began to wear a bit thin. Help came just when I needed it. I was attending a meeting of the representatives of the various missions who worked in Lebanon. I went as a representative of the Navigators. Each of us sat in a circle and as my turn came, I told what I was doing. Everyone had a 'product' to sell or a job to do but one man's report stood out as different from the rest. 'I'm here to impart a love for the Lebanese to my staff,' said the director of an agency. I thought to myself, 'This man I need to see!'

'Every missionary goes through three stages,' he said. 'First of all, it's all romantic, postcards of palm trees, photos of me on a camel, stories sent home telling of hospitality, so many new friends, exciting customs and culture. Then they go through a phase where, "Every Lebanese is a thief, a rogue or a liar," and sometimes all three put together. Finally they learn to love them just as they are. Let me explain.

'When you go to the market and you see a beautiful rug and ask the nice man how much it costs. "For you, my friend," he says, "it's a special price of just £15." Now you know that this rug would sell in England for twice the price at least. So the deal is done. However, when you get home you find that your Arab neighbour bought one for a quarter of the price you paid for yours. "I wuz robbed", you say. But did you pay the price that you thought was fair? "Well, yes." You see, in the Middle East an item is sold on the basis of what it's worth to the buyer whilst in the West it's sold at what it's worth to the seller. Not wrong, just different!'

This man's wise counsel also helped me to realise that I was judging my Arab friends from my Western, so-called Christian perspective. It took me some time to realise that each culture has its own strengths and weaknesses. When it comes to hospitality we can't hold a candle to the Arabic people. We may be quicker to clean up a mess, but would probably find the intrusion of guests into our lives harder to cope with.

One of the students took me up to his home in the northern part of Lebanon in the hills above the fertile plains of the Beka'a valley. We arrived at a very humble, typically whitewashed house, yellowed with age. I was treated like visiting royalty, especially by his mother. Many Lebanese prepare more food than is needed in case an unexpected friend or relative should turn up. There was a plentiful supply of olives and hommus. A speciality that I found very refreshing was a salad called *tabouleh* which was made up of crushed wheat, parsley, tomatoes and onions, doused in lemon juice. As appreciative as I was of the fine food and hospitality, eating 'sparrow' stew was a little difficult especially as the tiny bones had to be separated out as you ate them. Ugh!

We returned via the ancient temple city of Baalbeck. The Romans had transported the huge columns made of marble from their homeland. I have a snapshot in the family album showing me standing by one of Jupiter's columns. The base alone was taller than me! It was amazing to think that the temples were transported from such a great distance and erected without the powerful equipment we have today.

Another student invited me to visit his home in the southern port of Tyre which was once a very prosperous and powerful city. In fact it was considered to be impregnable. The reason the people felt so secure was that if an enemy came they would all retreat to an island off the coast, making invasion impossible. The invader would see sense and return home. Alexander the Great had better results. He destroyed the city and threw the rubble into the sea to make a causeway to the island. Today it is just a fishing village.

One of the highlights of the time in Tyre for me was being introduced to the famous Lebanese *mezzah*, a feast consisting of no fewer then twenty-four different dishes. I had to turn down the 'white stuff' when I was informed that it was sheep's brain. Another highlight was snorkling in the beautiful crystal clear Mediterranean. Alexander had obligingly left many fascinating ruins to see. Fragments of pottery, ancient tiles and ornamental carvings were there for the viewing.

The letters Sandra and I were writing daily at this time were a lifeline. I certainly missed her and especially would have liked her to share these experiences with me. Writing to each other was a new way to get to know one another – it gave us an opportunity to articulate our deepest thoughts and feelings. In one of my letters I casually mentioned that my haemoglobin had suddenly dropped, which was perhaps one of the first signs of oncoming health difficulties. Sandra immediately dispatched some iron tablets.

Sometimes things would remind me of England, especially films, and these made me wish I was there with her. The majestic views of the English countryside in the film *Far from the Madding Crowd* made me feel especially nostalgic and lonely for Sandra. Imagine my surprise when the fellow I had been to see the film with suddenly took my hand and held it as we walked down the street! I knew that Arab males were more affectionate with one another but I hadn't adjusted to the culture to that extent yet! I liked the way men greeted each other with a peck on the cheek but I wasn't ready for holding hands. In fact he didn't just hold my hand, he patted it as we walked along!

One of my final jobs before returning to Britain was helping a couple of American missionary ladies paint their flat. Sandra is forever grateful to them because they talked me into buying her a diamond engagement ring. Dutch people only buy one ring which is worn on the left hand when engaged and transferred to the right hand at the wedding ceremony. (Roman Catholics wear their rings the other way round.) I would just like to say that this custom has nothing to do with being tight-fisted!

This time of painting the flat was also part of a self-improvement programme. I felt that at my age it was time to grow up in my taste in music. Perhaps I should learn to appreciate classical music. I worked my way through the twelve records of the Reader's Digest, *Festival of Light Classical Music*. The powerful, dramatic strains of 'The Emperor', by Beethoven, finally clinched it for me. By definition Rock and Rollers of the fifties didn't like 'long hair' music as it was called in those days. 'Roll over Beethoven', sang Chuck Berry, but it was time for him to roll back now.

Time for me to head back to Sandra but not before a short detour via Israel. Because of a scheme allowing maximum mileage I was able to return to London via Cyprus and Tel Aviv. I didn't tell any of my Arab friends about this of course and went through the 'no passport stamp' queue so that there would be no evidence of my having been to Israel should I ever wish to return to Lebanon.

I stayed at the Church of the Holy Sepulchre hostel set in old Jerusalem, hidden away amongst the olive and pine trees. There were guided tours to the many interesting sights around the country. I travelled to Galilee by bus and was fed all the way on stuffed vine leaves by a kindly peasant lady. It was so special being in the land where Jesus walked and to get a feel for what life must have been like in those days so long ago. At the same time, seeing all the road signs being changed into Hebrew in the newly acquired occupied territories didn't bode well for the future. The Israelis were clearly planning on a long stay.

Finally, I arrived at a rainy Heathrow and set off to hitch-hike to Loughborough where Sandra was still staying. Nothing much had changed in my financial situation, since the last time when I arrived with 17s. 6d. in my pocket. When I arrived, Sandra was wearing a multicoloured, psychedelic dress that was in fashion at that time. She looked pretty bright but the love in her face shone even brighter. Boy, was I glad to be back!

A year later we would be married.

6

Marriage and Family (1969–75)

'In sickness and in health'

'Sandra, wilt thou have this man to thy wedded husband, to live together according to God's law in the holy estate of Matrimony? Wilt thou love him, comfort him, honour him and keep him, in sickness and in health; and, forsaking all other, keep thee only unto him, so long as ye both shall live?'

'I will.'

Something touched Sandra very deeply when the words 'in sickness and health' were spoken. 'What might this mean?' she thought to herself. The shadow that these words cast soon disappeared through the happiness of the marriage ceremony in a beautiful Victorian church in Manchester. All our friends and family had gathered for this glorious celebration. The church service closed with the hymn, 'Love divine all loves excelling', but we felt our love ran a close second to that divine love. After the service we went next door to the church hall for a reception.

Marriage and Family (1969–75)

We had the usual roast meal followed by the after-dinner speeches and toasts, but what followed gave the assembled guests a bit of a surprise, especially the English relatives. Our American best man, Lee Brase, introduced a rendition of 'This is our Lovely Day' sung by Miss 'Ambrosia Rice' and Miss 'Vesta Curry'. Poor Lee had no idea that their names were derived from pre-packaged food.

Our friend from Loughborough days, Robb Powrie Smith, told about our romance causing great hilarity to everyone there and embarrassing us as much as possible. The student music group who had serenaded us with 'Leaving on a Jet Plane' did so once again.

After the wonderful reception we were preparing to set off for our honeymoon only to find that my suitcase was locked in the jammed boot of someone's car. We thought at first that it was a practical joke but eventually the AA had to be called out to prise open the boot. Finally we set off in Sandra's dad's old VW 'Beetle'. My main memory of the day was that my face was sore from smiling so long! A bit like the cat that caught the canary.

We were going to spend the week of our honeymoon in a relative's caravan in Wales but decided to spend the first night in a hotel in Chester. We had booked months earlier and especially chosen a lovely room. 'Mr and Mrs van Zuylen here to book in, please.' It sounded good. We had been waiting such a long time to be able to introduce ourselves in this way. 'I'm sorry sir, but we have no booking under that name and in fact we are fully booked,' replied the receptionist. Was this a practical joke? There was no hint of a smile on his face. I insisted that we had been there three months earlier to select and book a room but to no avail. After some behind-the-scene discussions we were offered a small double room which was just about adequate. In fact it wasn't romantic at all. It was however, an opportunity for the young husband to show his new bride his resourcefulness. I wrapped the stark lighting in a towel which gave a lovely pink glow to the room. Very effective it was too, if I say so myself! As we began to make ourselves comfortable there was suddenly a flash and a loud bang. The light that I had so romantically decorated exploded and nearly burst into flames. You could say our honeymoon started off with a bang!

The next morning there was a knock on the door. Had we created a disturbance? A nervous new husband opened the door. 'Would you like a newspaper sir?' Being caught by surprise I asked him which ones he had, as if I knew the one from the other. The *News of the World* sounded reasonable so I asked for that one. I didn't know that this newspaper had so little 'news of the world', nor did I know that there would be rude pictures in it. Well, that's my story and I'm sticking with it! Sandra must have wondered what sort of interests this new husband had but in those days she was too trusting to ask.

We had a week of sun, laughter and tears. Starting off in the marriage relationship wasn't as easy as we had thought but at least we were together. We spent

Marriage and Family (1969–75)   55

the following week visiting friends before returning to Holland to set up our new home together in Groningen.

A year before our marriage, after my return from Lebanon we had both moved to Holland. I was invited by the Navigators to go to Groningen in the north of the country to start an evangelistic work amongst university students. Sandra went to the southern part of the country to learn Dutch at a convent language school in Vught.

Now, our new home together consisted of a kitchen, a lounge and a bedroom on the top floor of a three-storey building. The ground floor was a carpenter's workshop and the second floor was occupied by two students with whom we had to share a toilet. There was no bathroom at all, but fortunately there was a washbasin in the bedroom. Holland had a severe housing shortage so we were grateful for what we had.

We found the city that was now to be our home attractive with its bustling shopping centre, open market, gabled houses and the famous church tower known as the *Martinitoren*. Groningeners are known throughout the Netherlands for being dour but we found many of them welcoming and friendly. Our flat was located conveniently near to the main shopping area.

It was when we arrived at our new home in Groningen that we began to realise why the phrase, 'in sickness and health' had touched Sandra so deeply. Amongst the pile of cards and letters there was one requesting me to go into hospital for two weeks of tests in just three days' time!

I had donated blood the year before and as part of the routine check they give to every donor they had discovered that I had albumin in my urine. This meant that my kidney was malfunctioning, causing loss of protein that my body needed. Probably this accounted for my feeling more tired than usual over the past months. I had attributed this to the very busy schedule I had been keeping over the past year. Three days a week I had been working in a hardware warehouse earning my keep by stacking shelves, preparing orders and stocktaking. The other days were spent talking to students about their relationship to God.

We were able to delay the hospital visit for two weeks. When I was admitted to the renal ward I was introduced to a world I knew nothing of. What a sight some of the patients were on this ward! Some looked quite reasonable but others looked pale and jaundiced with hollow eyes. Dialysis was just being developed in a very crude and basic form that kept people barely alive. Whatever good it did them I don't know but it certainly scared me. As these patients were wheeled in after treatment I prayed that I would never need this.

One of the first things that was done on arrival in hospital was taking blood for various tests. A new doctor was being shown how to take blood from the hapless patient next to me. He was to try his newly acquired skill on me first. His hands were shaking and a bead of perspiration appeared on his brow as he came to take my blood. 'I'll just show you one more time,' said the senior doctor. The young doctor looked very relieved at the prospect but not half as much as I was!

The first in a series of tests to be done was a biopsy. A hollow needle was inserted into my back and into that went another needle to take out a sample of tissue from the kidney for analysis. The doctor doing the test was cursing under his breath because he couldn't get the needle through as easily as he had expected. 'Do you do a lot of sport?' he asked. 'You've got very tough muscles in your back.' 'No,' I said, 'but growing flowers involves doing a lot of bending and lifting and this has probably strengthened my muscles.' This compliment gave my deflated ego just the boost it needed!

One of my first visitors was the kindly minister of the church we attended. I had met him when I came to Groningen the previous year. I had visited him to introduce myself and inform him about the work I was hoping to do. After our chat he had walked over to his desk and spontaneously got out a Dfl. 25 note (about £10) and gave it to me to help with my costs. I was most touched by his generosity. 'You're in hospital for two reasons,' he said, 'for yourself, and to reach out to others.' I don't know whether I was much use to anyone else but for myself I came out with the diagnosis that I had some damaged kidney tissue, probably caused by an infection some years earlier. The prognosis was that my kidney function might stay the same or on the other hand it might eventually deteriorate. They couldn't say for sure. No particular treatment was prescribed and I didn't mind. I was only too glad to be out of hospital away from all those sick people. I didn't really take in the fact that my health could go seriously wrong. I had no time to be ill, there was too much to do.

As time went by I gradually began to get higher blood pressure and more severe migraines. I would need to stay in bed for one or two days a week, often being violently sick and unable to keep anything down. The number of students who often came to our house for spiritual guidance was increasing, so there was little time to think about what was happening to my health. I was able to give up my job at the warehouse so that I could work full-time with the students. This did not however decrease the workload because I did even more to use up all the available time. The group of people that I was overseeing had grown from one or two to over fifty in a little over a year. My mind was so full with the demands of the work around me. I didn't really take any time off and had no hobbies. We had quite an intense involvement in people's lives. Many hours were spent discussing deep issues with Dutch students who had strong opinions about most things and would express them quite forcibly. We weren't just talking to them about faith but also their deep concerns about relationships to parents or the opposite sex. Some were taking drugs or had significant needs concerning their self-worth.

Marriage and Family (1969–75)

It wasn't just a case of the burden of helping others either. I was quite hard on myself. I never felt I was doing enough or that what I was doing was good enough. The students didn't spare my sensibilities either. I remember one asking if he could see me. When we sat down he read from a prepared script what he felt were seven of my faults or should I say my 'seven deadly sins'. One I do remember well was that I tended to reject those who didn't agree with me. I had to admit that what he had observed was sometimes true.

I expressed to another that I often felt guilty and that I was never satisfied by what I had done. 'How do you think that makes us feel?' he replied, 'It makes us feel we can never do enough to please you!'

Often at night all these things would come back to me and I would spend futile hours thinking things over. I was eventually to learn that two in the morning is not a good time to do my evaluating. It's best just to have a nice little snack and go back to bed. Sometimes after a fried egg and a bit more sleep things would look better in the morning.

Sandra had taken a job in the pathology laboratory at the local hospital working as a medical technician. After a few months we were delighted to discover that Sandra was pregnant. Because I was at home during the daytime I was able to do a little more housework. On the front of our flat was a small balcony on which I hung out the washing but it was in full view of office workers across the road. To protect my embarrassment I used to hang the larger items in front of the 'smalls'. Sometimes I would drop something onto the pavement far below. My antics did seem to provide them with a little diversion from the boring office routine!

On April 19 our lovely daughter Mandy was born. It wasn't just me who thought that she was the most beautiful baby ever. Our minister, who had christened many babies said how exceptionally sweet she was, as he showed her to everyone at her christening! The birth had not been easy. Sandra was in labour for 28 hours. I was with her all of this time but when the birth was imminent I was sent out of the room. Hospital policy didn't allow the father to be present at the actual birth. The only way I was able to see anything was by watching through a keyhole in the door. I would quickly stand up if I heard any one approaching. I did actually catch a glimpse of Mandy as they lifted her up into view after the birth. I was soon let into the ward to sit with Sandra worshipping the fragile little creature that our love had made. Sandra, who had been silent throughout her ordeal wept gently as she exclaimed, 'She is so perfect, so beautiful.' I rode my bicycle back to our house in the April snow past the *Martinitoren*, the proudest man in all of Holland.

Our lives were greatly enriched by our new arrival, but my health continued to deteriorate. When Mandy was two months old we all went to a Navigator conference on the shores of Lake Geneva in Switzerland. The scenery was breathtaking and the stay at the hotel was a great break for us. The Swiss cheese fondue however couldn't be enjoyed by Sandra with me upstairs in bed with a blinding migraine. I didn't want people to know I was ill but it could be hidden no longer. 'How is Dirk?' a co-worker asked Sandra. She could conceal her concern no longer, and unable to get her words out she just wept and wept. There was no need to say anything, the tears communicated enough. The leadership of the Navigators decided it would be best for us to go to Britain to be under the care of a doctor who, because of his association with our work, knew more of the kind of pressure I was under. We gathered all our belongings into a borrowed VW bus, said goodbye to all our friends and headed for Britain into a very uncertain future.

Navigators in Britain found us a lovely bungalow in a little village on the outskirts of Guildford, called Jacob's Well. In the Bible this is the name of the place where Jesus met the Samaritan women to offer her water that would satisfy her forever. We certainly felt in need of refreshment.

I made regular visits to Dr Burton who prescribed plenty of rest. I was put on a mild sedative and medication to bring my blood pressure under control. Relaxing and enjoying life was not something that was easy for me to do. Sandra has a much greater capacity for enjoying life than I do and she was a great help. Mandy gave us endless entertainment with something new to enjoy every day. My horticultural instincts were able to find expression by doing some work on a garden nearby. It was also my first opportunity to visit the wonderful Royal Horticultural Society gardens at nearby Wisley.

Soon after we arrived, we received a letter from a lady we knew in Holland who had suffered much during the war. After five months of marriage her husband was taken away to a concentration camp and never heard of again. She suggested that a key to living in adverse circumstances was gratitude, thankfulness for what each day brought. We decided that at the end of each day we would thank God for the good that day had brought. Sometimes Sandra and I would just sit, not really feeling we could thank God at all! A recent visitor had said to us that the most important thing at a time like this was to believe in the sovereignty of God. In anger I thought, 'Of course I believe in the sovereignty of God! Who else got us into this situation?' The way I viewed the 'sovereignty of God' at that time was that he was simply exercising his irresistible will by placing us into a situation about which we had no choice. It took some time before I really began to understand that God always acts in love and wouldn't do anything to harm us even though he does allow unpleasant thing to happen. Nevertheless we did eventually find some peace in our hearts to thank him daily although our feelings did fluctuate a lot.

Our feelings were very much affected as we began to discuss our future with the Navigators. My suitability for the work was being questioned. 'Perhaps you don't have the necessary emotional stability.' It hurt deeply that somehow I was perceived to have failed. Shortly after we left Groningen someone had been brought in to take my place so it was clear to me that they didn't expect me to come back. I didn't know how to answer the question about my suitability; all I knew was that I loved the work that I had been doing.

So much of my security had been tied up in my work. I had become very unsure of myself now that I wasn't doing anything. I thought to myself, 'How can I be sure about teaching people? How will I know what is right?' Yet in considering what to do, there was nothing I would rather do than work with people and I felt I had been relatively successful. I joked with Sandra, 'Perhaps I could be a garbage collector' but she didn't think it was all that funny!

Gradually my health began to improve and an opportunity came up to go to Manchester, the city were we had been married, to work part-time, once again amongst students. And so we moved up North into a typical terraced two-up, two-down house. This quite amused us because before we left someone had said to us, 'I guess you will just have to move into a little terraced house if you go up there.' We had tried to assure her that not all the houses in Manchester were like that, but I don't think she was convinced.

A year later our first son, Mark, was born, a lively, fun-loving and mischievous lad from the start. Our stay in Manchester was not as long as we had expected because after two years we were asked to move to Sheffield to take responsibility for a thriving group of about thirty students.

During this time migraines persisted, if less frequently, and medicine to control blood pressure was needed. There was relative stability in the kidney function. Transplantation was becoming more commonplace and I assumed that if anything went wrong I would just walk into a hospital and get a new or should I say second-hand kidney.

7

The Kidney Machine (1976)

'Chiquitita'
Abba

At the beginning of 1976 our world suddenly seemed to collapse. I experienced a number of distressing symptoms which I assumed were side effects of the drugs I was taking. I explained to the doctor the new symptoms of nausea, lack of energy and an itchy skin rash. To my complete surprise she didn't make the expected change of medicine but informed me that my kidney was failing completely. Dr Platt explained that I would need to go onto a kidney machine before long. Though I was in a state of shock I remember her saying that I would need to spend seven hours a day, three days a week on a machine which would be placed in an especially equipped room in our house. If we didn't have enough space indoors a Portacabin could be placed behind our house. There would also be a very strict and restricted diet. When making tentative enquiries about my life expectancy she replied, 'Well you can't expect to live as long as most people!' I was devastated. At thirty-one the dark shadows from the past had become reality.

An appointment was made at the hospital to have a fistula operation that would make 'dialysis' possible. Haemodialysis is the process whereby the blood is purified and excess fluid removed by an artificial kidney.

A vein and an artery were to be surgically joined together in my arm. This would cause the vein to swell thereby increasing the blood supply needed for the treatment. Listening to my arm with the stethoscope after the operation the doctor exclaimed, 'It sounds like a train rushing through there!' One of my bizarre party tricks was to have someone place their hand on my pulse. This usually gave them quite a shock as they could feel it throbbing so powerfully. Some were allowed to have a listen as well! Sandra however, didn't much like the sound of my 'rushing train' under her pillow keeping her awake at night!

One day after a visit to the clinic, I returned home to find the house empty, with a note saying that Sandra had taken three-year-old Mark to the children's hospital for immediate admission. She had taken him to our GP that morning having smelled acetone on his breath. She had a vague memory from her time of working in the hospital that there was some connection between this substance and diabetes. The doctor confirmed Sandra's impression and indeed Mark did have diabetes and needed immediate treatment to get things under control.

The Kidney Machine (1976)

We had been wondering for a while what was happening to him. He had gradually changed from a very lively lad who wouldn't sit still for a moment, to one who would happily sit on my knee for a cuddle. This was rather nice so we had assumed that Mark was just growing up and settling down a bit as children do. His constant thirst and return to wetting the bed at night however, were more concerning.

It was a great comfort to us that Mark was admitted to a ward where our good friend Gill Stiles was the sister in charge. In this bewildering environment he was very hard to control and it was a daunting and distressing place for us to visit as well, made more so by seeing the often greater suffering of other children and their parents. We were all finding it very difficult to understand and accept the situation he was in.

Gill told us that when Mark had been in hospital for about two weeks he came into her office one day and talked about a few inconsequential things. Suddenly he said, 'I won't have to do injections when I go home, will I?' She explained that he would have to do them when he got home and for the rest of his life. He persisted in repeating the same question several times and she replied that he would have to do them at home and for always. Mark then broke down and sobbed, clinging onto her for several minutes. They cried together. He then took a deep breath, stopped crying and went into the ward. That night he did his own injection for the first time. It was as though he fought against the diabetes while he was talking to her and then told himself that if this is how it is going to be then he was going to cope with it.

Before Mark went home both Sandra and I also had to learn how to measure out the insulin and help with injections. Sandra had been coming in regularly to do this but I was very reluctant to get involved. Gill felt she had to face me about this. On the next visit she asked me to come into her office and insisted that I give Mark his injection. 'You are not leaving here until you do his injection!' she said. I was very angry but did as she asked.

I well remember him doing his first injections himself while in hospital. He would take the needle in his hand and move towards his leg, his little hand shaking all the while. Suddenly he would say something quite unrelated to what he was doing as he built up his courage. Gathering up his nerve he moved his needle a little closer to his leg and then pinched up the skin with his left hand and said, 'I played with my new car today.' His shaky hand was now holding the needle against his skin and in it went, his face wincing a little. Then off he went into the ward looking for a little friend to play with.

When Mark returned from hospital shortly after this he was soon his usual speedy self but he wasn't so willing to do his own injections. One injection each morning required some pretty fast footwork by me as I chased him through the house. I remember sometimes needing to literally sit on him as he squirmed trying to get away from the dreaded needle. I wasn't in that good shape myself with quite a low haemoglobin and was devastated at having to do this. Sandra was not particularly fit either being eight months pregnant!

'How can God allow this to happen to such a little kid?' I said to Sandra in bed one night and began weeping. This was the first time I had cried since becoming an adult. I can still picture the scene sitting up in bed together looking at our seventies-style flower-meadow pattern on the wall opposite. The comfort and pleasantness of the location almost mocked our sorrow. Life felt so bleak. Life was anything but a flower-filled meadow! I think our pain and turmoil was accentuated because we felt that as full-time Christian workers God should give us some special favour and protection.

We did feel it was divine providence that we became acquainted with a student called Kim Pollard. He too was diabetic but his enthusiasm, his active sports life and his kindness attracted Mark. In fact in many ways Kim became his role model. They would often talk and sometimes Mark would ask him questions about diabetes. Sometimes Kim would let Mark watch as he gave himself his injection. Mark wanted to do his injections himself just like Kim so at three years old he started doing his injections again all by himself. I had never heard of anyone so young doing this.

He had his ups and downs though. Sometimes he would have very severe headaches and 'helpful' comments like, 'diabetes is nothing these days' would touch the anger and helplessness in my soul. The deepest sorrow I experienced was kneeling beside his bed powerless to do anything about the pain he was experiencing.

We had to make many adjustments because of my imminent renal failure and Mark's diabetes, one of which was our diets. Mark needed to have the right amount of carbohydrate at frequent intervals. Sugary things were forbidden unless his blood sugar suddenly went too low, indicated by his face looking a deathly white colour. My own diet was very different being restricted in substances the failing kidney had difficulty coping with. Protein-rich foods such as meat and cheese were restricted, as were salty foods like bacon and most tinned foods. I felt that the dieticians seemed to see us as human chemical factories who had no preferences, or taste buds for that matter. A fear of potassium-rich food like bananas and mushrooms was instilled into us kidney patients. In fact all fresh fruit and vegetables were restricted. Even potatoes needed to be soaked before boiling to remove some of the offending potassium. Chips were out unless they were boiled first. Fluid too was restricted because of the kidneys' limited ability to handle liquids. Wine, beer or any drink with fruit content was not allowed, again because of potassium. We were told horror stories of patients who had died because of neglecting their diet. Even though Sandra had been trained in measuring out amounts of chemicals in her work in the lab, nothing prepared her for the complications of our very different diets.

It embarrasses me to write this, but all this time I was trying to carry on with my life and work as if nothing was happening, trying to take everything in my stride. Sandra particularly had to bear the brunt of this. We had a very busy home during this time, as always. People were visiting frequently and we even had three people living with us who were there to help in the student work and to receive training in Christian ministry. My health was rapidly deteriorating but I wasn't really aware of the effect this was having on Sandra.

It took a visit from my mother to sort me out! Sandra couldn't easily talk to me about how she felt because I was part of the problem. During the time with us my mother asked if we were coping, to which I answered, 'Yes, we're managing all right'. At this point Sandra could contain her feelings no longer and suddenly began to scream! I was staggered, she had never, ever done this before! Only then did it begin to dawn on me how much the pressure of the situation was affecting her but I didn't know what to do and was reluctant to make any changes to our lifestyle.

'You must reduce the pressure in your home,' my mother said, 'It's too much for Sandra.' I didn't like her telling me how to run my own home and anyway my philosophy was that you just cope. If things are difficult there is nothing you can do but just press on. I had to admit, however, that she was right and I needed to take notice of her advice. I asked the people who were staying with us to find somewhere else to stay and of course they were more than willing to do so. We also arranged to have fewer activities in our home.

My mother's being there was in fact courtesy of our Navigator student group in Sheffield. People showered us with kindness. Some sent cards, others gifts and still others books of poetry. (Not that I liked poetry much at that time, but it's the thought that counts.) Some people phoned and others let us know that they didn't phone because they knew we would be inundated with calls.

We did not sense God's love in our family health situation at all but our friends were very loving towards us. The love of friends is very tangible; it can be seen and felt. We began to see that God was expressing his love to us through these people. Ultimately, this helped us to see God's love for us. The lessons learned through this traumatic time stayed with us through the difficult days that were to come. Before this time I considered people to be important but now I realised I couldn't survive without the help of friends.

One of the things that wasn't so helpful however were the books well-meaning people sent us on healing. These writers assumed that God would heal. 'You just needed to accept it by faith.' If you weren't healed, they argued, it was because you didn't believe or there was some sin stopping you. What was disturbing about this was that, by implication, your difficulties are your own fault because you don't trust God enough.

The Kidney Machine (1976)

Generally speaking people around us were very supportive but the inevitability of the kidney machine was coming closer and closer. I needed to prepare myself for this and so it was suggested that I should visit someone who had dialysing facilities at home. I arranged to visit a local man who had his kidney treatment room behind his grocer's shop. It frightened me seeing his situation so I asked him, 'How do you cope?' 'Well, it's this or t' church yard,' he said in his broad Yorkshire accent. I guess you can't make it any clearer than that!

On March 29 Stephen was born. What a timely gift! He was such an easy-going baby and gave us a welcome focus away from the family traumas. I particularly remember his bright eyes and his happy smile. He had lovely blond curls that Sandra particularly was very reluctant to cut when he became older.

Before starting with the kidney machine I wanted to make one final visit to my family in Holland. I had been told that holidays would be limited in the future, because there was really no break possible once dialysis started. The doctors suggested dialysing once in the hospital to clean up my blood, as it were, before going. I went to the old Royal Hospital in Sheffield town centre to get my first treatment. I got into the bed in a room that had windows but no view and had very dim lighting. The nurse had got everything ready and so I simply needed to extend my fistula arm for her to put in the needles, one to withdraw and the other to return the blood that was being treated in the artificial kidney. It is of course, quite an unnatural way to purify my blood and so my body reacted to the treatment. 'You're a brave man,' said the nurse, as I was being sick into the recycled-paper bowl. I didn't feel very brave. My head ached and my stomach retched but it was over. My first dialysis. Was this what life was going to be like from now on?

The five of us piled into our white Hillman estate and set off for the Hull-Rotterdam ferry, anxious to show off our new offspring to the family. We had a great time visiting many of the tourist sights in Holland. They all loved a wonderful park called the *Efteling* where the rides and buildings are all based around fairy tales. The wonderful sandy beaches not far from where my parents live were often visited. One of the pleasant things we were able to do was to sit having coffee and *apelgebak* (appletart) on the seafront while the children were safely playing at the water's edge enjoying the waves rolling in. It was over all too soon.

Back in Britain we nearly had a bad accident. I was driving along when I saw a lorry coming towards us on our side of the road. I suddenly thought, 'I'm on the wrong side of the road,' and swerved to the right. He continued on the same side of the road. It was only as we passed that I realised what had happened. We had passed each other on the wrong side of the road! Shaking with nerves I pulled over to the kerb as it began to dawn on me what a narrow escape we had had, due to my confusion. Being disoriented from driving on the other side of the road in Holland I had incorrectly assumed I was on the wrong side of the road. The lorry driver had simply been pulling out to overtake someone. 'You take over,' I said to Sandra.

I was so sick and nauseous on the way back that I had to get out of the car from time to time to get some fresh air. Sandra drove me straight to the hospital to begin treatment. My body was full of poisons that needed dialysing out as soon as possible.

The strategy in those days was to let the kidney deteriorate to the point of being at 'death's door' so that the patient really appreciates the treatment when he gets it. I was grateful, if not very alive!

Lodge Moor was formerly a TB isolation hospital that had been brought back into service as a renal dialysis unit. (One of the reasons for locating here was the danger of the spread of Hepatitis B which had caused deaths in the renal units of other hospitals.)

It wasn't just me that was run down, the hospital itself looked in need of urgent treatment too but its location on the edge of the city overlooking beautiful moorland was charming indeed. It was June and the weather was balmy but I can't say that I really paid much attention to this as I entered the unit. 'Abba' music drifted over from the transistor radios.

> Chiquitita, tell me what's wrong,
> You're enchained by your own sorrow.
> In your eyes, there's no hope for tomorrow,

The renal unit, once I had found it in what seemed like a maze of corridors, was divided into two parts.

One side had sleeping accommodation and the other was for dialysis with a small morning room alongside. There were ten beds for treatment, five on each side of the ward looking as stark as only a Victorian hospital can.

I was shown to a bed in the middle of the ward and placed my few personal belongings into the bedside cabinet. The first thing that needed to be learned was how to work with the kidney machine and how dialysis works.

What was it that the nurse had said? 'First of all you prime the system with saline and then you set the heparin pump so that your blood doesn't clot. Insert the venous and arterial needles into your fistula arm being sure to clamp off the attached line first. Before you do that it will help if you inject lignocaine under your skin so it won't hurt so much. Now you are ready to connect the needle to the venous line. Slowly start the blood flow by switching on the blood pump being sure to release the clamp from the line first. The saline in the arterial line can be drained away until traces of blood show. Now you can connect the line to your body completing the circuit. Got that?'

Next to my bed was not a 'Dalek' sent to exterminate, though it looked a bit like it, but the kidney machine. On the front panel there were a number of dials measuring the temperature, pressure and flow of the dialysate fluid, amongst other things. The most threatening alarm on the machine was the one which indicated that blood was seeping into the dialysate fluid. A red light came on and an irritating bleeping noise began. If this happened the dialysis procedure needed to start all over again.

The artificial kidney or dialyser as it is usually called was connected to the machine and to the fistula in my arm. The dialyser is the piece of equipment which actually cleaned my blood and is separate from the machine. It is a semi-permeable membrane made of cellulose. The dialyser is so designed that blood passes across one side of the membrane and a specially prepared dialysing solution passes in the opposite direction at the other side. The membrane allows impurities and excess fluids in the blood to pass through and be carried away in the dialysate solution, but the blood cells are too large to pass through the pores. This was the part that did the actual purifying of the blood. Put simply, dialysis is the process of purifying blood and removing excess fluid, working by osmosis.

Little by little my passing of urine decreased until it stopped completely. I was now totally dependent on a machine to stay alive!

Nurses on the renal unit are a special breed. I see them more as trainers than nurses. They are very dedicated to getting the best out of their patients. Nothing seems to please them more than if they can get a kidney patient back into normal life as soon as possible.

On my first day there was a nurse standing near the end of my bed pointing to something on the floor. 'Who spilt this blood?' she barked! Some poor soul who had just dialysed and had that typical zombie look about him meekly owned up. 'Well clean it up!' she commanded, gave me a wink and said to me 'That's the way we treat 'em around here.' I got the message.

It was interesting to see how the different patients coped with the life-threatening predicament they were in. In the bed next to me was Mr Mind-Over-Matter. Problems were there to be overcome. He freely advised the rest of us on how to deal with any difficulty we had. On the other side was the pathetic, 'I just want to die' person. He felt that no one was suffering like he was even though we were all in the same situation. Across the way was Mr Angry. Angry at everyone and about everything, the food, the staff but strangely not expressing any anger directly about his own illness.

One patient, Mavis, whom I got to know quite well, had a smile and kind words for others even though she was desperately ill. Her renal failure was a complication of child-birth. She never had the chance to get to know her new baby because she died shortly after going home.

I don't know what my own reaction was. At first I was too ill to feel anything and later had a sense of 'I can't believe this is happening to me.' I was, however, encouraged by a visit by my favourite nurse Hazel. She came and sat down by my bed and asked me, 'Who do you represent?' I was quite puzzled by this. I could have said, 'I represent Jesus' but would have seemed a little presumptuous and I might have felt a little foolish saying that. Not really waiting for a reply she said, 'I've got ESP and I know that you're different!' I was somewhat thrown by this as I certainly didn't feel any different. I knew I looked different after losing more than a stone since starting dialysis but that wasn't what she meant! From my point of view I found putting in the large needle, the sickness and the cramps hurt me as much as anyone else. My faith was not an anaesthetic! Then she clarified what she meant, 'You have peace,' she said. Through what she said I realised that my faith in God had made a difference.

The question, 'Who do you represent?' had come from the hospital form I filled in stating my occupation as 'representative'. There hadn't been any room to write that I was a Navigator.

For the initial six weeks of dialysis I had to stay in hospital all the time, but for the following five I was able to go in only for the dialysis sessions. The weather was so beautiful during these weeks, it just didn't seen right to be going into a hospital! Sandra needed to accompany me so that together we could learn the techniques and procedures necessary for home dialysis. Connecting and disconnecting me from the machine had to be learnt, also how to deal with emergencies such as blood leaks in the artificial kidney, or falling blood pressure. We felt very fearful at the prospect of having so much complex equipment in our home and being solely responsible for everything. Sandra's coming into the hospital for training was significantly complicated by the fact that she was still breast feeding three-month-old Stephen at the time. This meant that feeding had to be fitted in around the twice-daily hospital visits. Thankfully Stephen was a contented and happy baby. There were so many different things to adjust to at the same time that she often felt quite overwhelmed.

Difficult as it was, we were glad that I was still alive. There were ten of us to start with on the ward; by the end of the summer, three had died.

8

Life on Dialysis (1976–77)

'One day at a time'
Lena Martell

'A hospital room in the comfort of your own home.' A hospital, but with very inexperienced staff, part of our home, but intruding drastically into the lifestyle of those living there. Home dialysis was all part of a strategy to provide the patient with opportunity to live as normal a life as possible.

A bedroom in our home was converted to be used for dialysis with all the equipment I needed. The especially built shelves lining the room were packed full of boxes of medicines, needles, syringes of various sizes, boxes of bandages and sterilised lines for connecting to and from the artificial kidney to the machine. Bags of sterilised saline and dextrose solution for intravenous administration weighed down the top shelf. The newly laid waterproof floor was piled high with boxes containing Renalyte, sterilising fluid and burnbins to dispose of infected material. Lorry loads of supplies were delivered from the hospital on a regular basis. On the wall there were electrical plugs specially fitted from a separate electricity supply to connect to the kidney machine, de-ioniser and blood pump and any other needs. In the far corner was a large sink used for washing the artificial kidney. The water came from a separate mains supply because a loss in water pressure would make dialysis impossible. On one side of my bed was a small table and on the other the kidney machine which controlled the artificial kidney or 'dialyser' alongside it. This contraption was about eighteen inches wide, four foot long and eight inches thick, made up of four large plastic plates with semi-porous membranes between each layer. The health service electricians had installed two pullcords hanging from the ceiling within arm's reach of where I sat, one for the lights and another to set off an emergency alarm system. (Sandra learned to hate that sound.) One other essential piece of equipment in the room was the television, absolutely vital for distraction during the seven-hour procedure.

The machine would need to be switched on in the morning to warm up and to run all the necessary checks. After an hour or so I would go into the room to get everything ready. The artificial kidney needed to have the sterilising solution rinsed out and replaced with saline. This always had to be done with great care as the 'formalin' used for sterilising is lethal stuff. Lines used for carrying the blood around the system needed to be primed ready for use. Finally I prepared the table. First of all I cleaned it with disinfectant. I

Life on Dialysis (1976–77)

needed to take great care to avoid dangerous contamination of the sterilised equipment so I wore a clean gown, plastic gloves and a paper face mask. Then I filled a syringe with lignocaine to anaesthetise my skin and two larger needles were prepared, one for the supply of blood for treatment and another to return the purified blood to my body. I would then weigh myself to see how much fluid I had accumulated since the last dialysis, and then take my blood pressure.

I was finally ready to begin the dialysis, so Sandra was called to give assistance. She too had to make sure no bacteria entered the process, so after carefully washing her hands she had to wear gloves, face mask and a clean plastic apron. Sandra would then hand me the pieces of equipment as I needed them. First of all I would sterilise my skin ready for inserting the needles. Usually this went well but sometimes my vein could be accidentally punctured, 'blown' we called it. This caused severe swelling of my arm and sometimes rendered dialysis impossible. It was always a very tense time and I would sometimes get snappy with Sandra. It all felt so unnatural, so technical, even surreal. My wife was a nurse who couldn't nurse me: a helper who passed instruments that hurt me. If she made a mistake she could cause me harm. There was a sense of relief when the connecting-up procedure passed with no particular problems.

During the first few hours I would usually feel well, greatly cheered by the arrival of my favourite food. Let me explain.

Renal failure brings with it the need for a very strict diet. Drinking is restricted in order to limit the build-up of fluid in the body between treatments. Salt is restricted because of its fluid-attracting property. I was surprised how many foods contain salt. The only cereal allowed was Shredded Straw – sorry – Wheat. 'Bet you can't eat three.' Protein is restricted because of the way it causes dangerous impurities to build up in the system. Potassium is restricted because too much of this in the body can cause a heart attack. Chocolate is strictly *verboten*.

Officially the doctors and nurses didn't allow any breaking of these rules but word got around that what was eaten whilst on dialysis was dialysed out before it could do any harm. 'Well, that's my theory and I am sticking to it!' As long as the dietician didn't find out, you were OK. 'Didn't they know that it is a scientifically proved fact eating chocolate effects your well-being? Ask any woman!'

If I dialysed in the morning my favourite meal was a full English breakfast: bacon, eggs, mushrooms, HP sauce. If I dialysed in the afternoon it would be pizza with as many toppings as possible: pepperoni, cheese, more mushrooms, and tomato. A cold glass of beer was enjoyed with this. I used to sit there in my bed, attached to the machine I hated, but smiling to myself. I felt I understood Adam and Eve a lot better. It's not what you *are* allowed but what you *aren't* that you really want!

One time when attending a party at James and Mary Fox's house where everyone was having pizza,

Life on Dialysis (1976–77)

Mary had kindly prepared some steak for me, of which a small amount was actually allowed on my diet. Everyone was making comments about what a lucky fellow I was. I couldn't explain that I would have much rather had the same as the rest of them.

I would usually pass the time on the machine reading, starting off with the Bible and then novels or true-life stories. James Herriot is just the man to take your mind off things. The only danger is falling out of your bed with laughter! Gradually as concentration became more difficult I would then be reduced to watching daytime television. (You know how bad someone's feeling when they are reduced to watching daytime television. I never got so bad that I watched game shows.) Having said that, I did enjoy watching old films, especially Humphrey Bogart classics and British films like 'Brief Encounter', through which I discovered Rachmaninov.

As the dialysis progressed I would gradually feel the side-effects. I would become tired and weak, developing a headache quite different from a normal one. Something far deeper seemed to take place. I can only describe it as a feeling of wanting to hide within myself to recover. Noise and light were especially difficult to cope with. I would be watching the clock waiting for the seven hours to pass so Sandra could be called to help me to disconnect from the machine.

Sometimes disconnecting had to occur prematurely. It didn't happen often, but sometimes impurities would get into the system. The first time this happened it was quite alarming. The first symptom of a 'rigor' as it is called, would be that I would begin to feel shivery. I would ask Sandra for an extra blanket. When this didn't help, Sandra phoned the hospital doctor. After she explained what was happening he told her, 'Get in touch again if you are concerned.' Time passed and the symptoms were getting worse and I was now shaking quite violently and unable to get warm no matter how many blankets were piled on top of me. Once again Sandra phoned and explained the developments. Once again the doctor told her to get in touch if she was worried. 'I *am* worried, that's why I'm phoning you!' He finally got the picture and told Sandra to get me off the machine and to try it again the next day.

Disconnecting from the machine was always a tense affair, especially in the early days. It had been drummed into us during our training that one of the biggest dangers was getting air in the line. If air entered the system and as a result my body, I could die. 'One foot of air can kill you,' the nurse had said. Even though there was a phone in the room to call the hospital in emergencies there was a great sense of inadequacy and fear. One afternoon Sandra suddenly became very ill with flu and just couldn't get out of bed. Eight-year-old Mandy had to help me disconnect, a clamp at the ready should any air get into the system. In fact the only time any air did get into the system and was within a few inches of entering my body was when a doctor friend offered to help so that Sandra could have a break! What was that joke about only doctors being able to 'bury their mistakes'?

Life on Dialysis (1976–77)

After disconnecting at two or three kilos lighter then when I started, and feeling tense, the artificial kidney had to be sterilised for use the next time. The worst thing was on testing the kidney to find that one of the fragile membranes had ruptured and needed replacing. This was a time-consuming and precise procedure. After everything was cleaned up I usually had a bath which always seemed to do more then just clean the outside of my body. It was almost like a ceremonial cleansing from contact with a defiling object. Some food would usually aid the recovery process though it wasn't much fun for the family having me sit at table. I would rarely socialise with anyone outside the family, usually heading for bed fairly early. I felt fragile, my nerves on edge. A headache was compounded by inner feelings of vulnerability and sadness. I would sometimes seek comfort from Sandra's body but was usually sexually impotent. Sleep was very deep on dialysis nights which was a welcome change from the usual pattern of sleeping difficulties.

The next morning I would wake up feeling good and ready to try and get on with normal life.

'We don't want you to see yourself as an invalid!' The nurses and doctors worked very hard to get me back into normal living as soon as possible. Quite a strong bond develops between staff and patient because of the regular contact. The dedication of the staff and their concern for my welfare was, and is, very special indeed. Nothing seemed to please them more than to know that I was working again. The goal seemed to be to learn how to live with dialysis as a long-term solution. Even a transplant was considered only a 'holiday from dialysis' at that time.

I couldn't wait to get back to work. Even in the hospital I had continued to see people and this carried on once I arrived home. Sometimes I would counsel people whilst dialysing. Some were so impressed by the technology involved that they would wax eloquent on the wonders of modern science. Though I did agree I would sometimes unkindly think, 'Why don't you try it if you think it's so great?' With others I noticed a distinct loss of colour in their faces as they focused on the maze of tubes and the needles into my arm, and asked to be excused.

In fact *my* colour had gradually changed too. My skin had taken on the distinctive colour of putty because of the anaemia and impurities in my system. My lips too became paler. One day as I was walking down the Moor in Sheffield a stranger came up to me and said, 'You're a kidney patient, aren't you?' 'Yes I am. How can you tell?' I replied. 'I can tell by your *look*.'

It was difficult for me to accept that so much of my life was taken up with my health problems. Even though I tried to keep on working, obviously there were limitations. It took me a while to accept that I was actually at work part-time and that didn't mean squeezing six days' work into three! Bob Croson commented at the time, 'I get tired just watching you!' and there were plenty of jokes about the 'Flying Dutchman' too.

Life on Dialysis (1976–77)

One day a woman with whom we had only passing contact phoned up and asked to speak to me. 'I just can't get the words of a Bible verse out of my mind and I have to share it with you: *I will restore to you the years that the swarming locusts have eaten.* I don't know exactly what it means but I feel I should share it with you.'

Was this God's way of telling us that the time lost by the 'locust' – dialysis would somehow be made up to us? We didn't know, but this prophesy gave us hope.

In fact it had become apparent that I could not really carry on leading the student group of over 100 people. It was suggested by the Navigators that I take on a more supervisory role with other student leaders in the North of England. James Fox was in Leeds, Peter Dowse, who took over from me, was in Sheffield and Thompy Wright was in Newcastle and now married to nurse Gill Stiles. Although I was very fond of these people I found this very hard to take because I felt I was being kicked upstairs.

I very much enjoyed the day-to-day contact with students, talking to them about real-life issues. It was exciting to see lives changed as their relationship and loyalty to Christ strengthened. Some years earlier I had felt overlooked in not being given more responsibility but now I was very satisfied by my work and felt suited to it. It seemed to me a little like being put out to pasture but, as time went by, I gradually settled into this new role made all the more enjoyable by the fine people I worked with.

There were not only adjustments to work patterns but also to our whole lifestyle. People would often say to me, 'Well, you just need to live a day at a time.' In fact, there was a popular song around at the time by one-hit wonder Lena Martell called, 'One Day at a Time'. To be truthful, I didn't know what the phrase meant, but gradually I began to realise it actually meant *enjoying* one day at a time. I needed to enjoy what each day had to bring. If a friend came along I could enjoy being with him or her. If the weather was good, I could enjoy that. When I am working I find pleasure in my work. It was easy to let difficulties spoil the good there was to be found. One of the hardest lessons for me to learn is to enjoy what I'm actually doing rather than only the finished product. The phrase, 'It's better to travel then to arrive', had no place in my vocabulary. During this time I took up gardening and it was especially here that I noticed my attitude to work the most. If I couldn't finish what I started in the time allocated I would get very frustrated. I needed to learn to enjoy the work itself. If I'm digging enjoy the digging. I mustn't let my pleasure be spoiled by feeling I have to finish the job right away.

I began to realise that I needed to enjoy our children more too. One day when I was feeling quite depressed, Stephen asked me to play with him. Reluctantly, I joined him in kicking a ball around. To my surprise my depression had lifted after our little game. He was a real help to me being such a bright cheerful little fellow who had a smile for everyone. Just like his dad – not!

Life on Dialysis (1976–77)

Mark was a typical lad. He enjoyed sports, especially football and especially Manchester United. There wasn't much quality football in Sheffield in those days. He loved to imitate what he saw the students doing. After a walk in the beautiful Peak District, not far from our house, he had noticed climbers on the rock faces and felt he could give this a go on our stairs as well. So, kitted out with an ice-cream container as a helmet and some size 10 boots he had borrowed, he was observed hanging from the banister on the end of a blue climbing rope.

Mandy's interests were numerous. She went to Brownies, she played violin and piano. Usually her best friend Rebecca would be over, playing with Tiny Tears. She loved sports too, especially gymnastics, and would often be seen giving impromptu performances for whoever she could find to watch. Something very special for her was when our cat Kiki gave birth to five kittens in our upstairs bedroom.

One of the things we tried to do as a family and sometimes as a couple was to get away from the house for a weekend or longer if possible. Holiday possibilities were very limited because there were few facilities for kidney patients. Once we went away to a cottage in Windermere that had dialysing facilities in a Portacabin next door. It was nice for the children but of course it was no real break from dialysis, not for me or Sandra. On occasion I was allowed to take a three-day break and so we would go to a hotel for a few days of luxury. It was great to get away to be together and try to forget everything for a while. It wasn't as easy as we would have liked. Every mealtime I would cheat a little on my diet and Sandra would be afraid that something serious would happen. The salty foods would increase my thirst and I would then sneak out to an ice machine in the corridor to quench it. During a weekend like that I would gain as much as four kilos fluid weight! This was strictly forbidden and would all need to come off at the next dialysis – not good.

At Lodge Moor Hospital they were seeking to develop a portable kidney machine which was one of the first of its kind and I was thrilled to be the first to be allowed to take it on holiday with me.

The BSI (British Information Service) got wind of this and wanted to do a publicity film for international distribution to show British technological developments. So off the five of us went to rural Derbyshire to shoot the film at a cottage. Lights! Action! Camera! Shots were taken of the children playing outside while I pretended to use the new machine inside the cottage with Sandra helping me. It was great fun and after it was released it was quite surprising to receive letters from colleagues in other countries like Jordan and Singapore, who had seen the film. Fame at last!

9

Sandra's Perspective (1979)

'Behold and see'
Handel's Messiah

Sandra was asked by a national magazine to write down her thoughts about what life was like for her with a husband dependant on a machine to live. She wrote:

Very soon my husband will be returning from a weekend away. I've just switched on his kidney machine ready for him to dialyse as soon as he comes home. I feel a tug inside at the thought of not being able to spend the evening with him relaxing. At the same time I am thankful that he is able to do so much and that the machine has kept him in reasonable health for three years now.

Dialysis occurs three times every week usually from 3:30 pm until 9:30 pm. On most occasions everything goes smoothly. I connect Dirk to the machine, bring him his meals and disconnect him six hours later. Sometimes dialysis doesn't go smoothly. I may be putting the children to bed when the bell from the kidney room rings. I go to the room and find Dirk struggling with breathing and experiencing cramps in his legs. This is due to a sudden fall in blood pressure. I quickly introduce a bag of saline and run it in until Dirk feels better. Another time I'm in the middle of preparing a meal when the alarm bell rings. I run upstairs to find the machine bleeping and the knob marked Blood Leak flashing. 'Oh no, he's just started dialysing.' Now he has to be disconnected, the artificial kidney cleaned and reassembled. We wait for two hours for it to sterilise and then start again. 'Oh Lord,' I think, 'why does life have to be so hard?'

The next day the door to the kidney room is closed, and we can have a normal day ... that is, apart from starting the day with Mark's injection of insulin at 7:30 am and counting his carbohydrates at every meal ... that is, apart from watching the clock to make sure his meals and snacks are on time ... that is, apart from wondering what interesting meals I can prepare for Dirk without the aid of salt, tinned meats and vegetables, stock cubes, cheese and only limited amounts of fruit and vegetables.

At the end of a busy day we fall into bed. Half an hour later Dirk gets up, has something to eat, reads a newspaper or book and returns to bed; eventually he falls into a fitful sleep, often thrashing out with his legs (restless legs syndrome, they call it). 'Oh, Lord, it's so hard to watch my loved ones suffer.'

After three years of this kind of life we are discovering that despite difficulties there is much in life that makes it worth living. We have many things to be

Sandra's Perspective (1979)

thankful for and God is with us in the midst of difficulties. Oh yes, the superficiality has been rubbed away, the pat answers which we easily gave to other people are gone, and left underneath is the very basis of our faith.

Do I really believe Jesus or not? Do I trust him and believe that he is in complete control? Do I believe that 'his strength is made perfect in weakness'?

If the Christian life were dependent upon what I do for God I would fail miserably, but thank God it is dependent on what he has done and is doing for me. I have felt like a 'bruised reed' and 'a dimly burning wick', but he has not quenched me but is restoring and healing me.

The circumstances of the past four years have brought many attitudes to the surface which I didn't realise were in me.

Self-pity rears its ugly head so often as I allow myself to dwell on my lot in life and how difficult it is. This train of thought very quickly leads to depression and gloom. I am learning to thank God for all the good things he has given us (e.g. Dirk and Mark are alive and well), and to dwell on the fact that God loves us and his love for us is perfect in every way, even if it involves suffering.

I have found myself feeling angry with God because he has allowed things to come into our lives which I did not want or ask for. It has helped to express these rebellious feelings to Dirk or a close friend who will listen and not think, 'All is lost,' if I say outrageous things.

Then I've needed to spend some time alone with God and pour it all out to him, realising that nothing I can do can change the circumstances. He has brought peace as I've submitted to his sovereignty. He has given me assurance that his grace is sufficient for me, that his presence is with me at all times and his provision will meet my needs. Yet I have doubted God's love as I have asked, 'Why have you allowed these things to happen if you love us?'

The Lord encouraged us through Psalm 34:18–20 (*Living Bible translation*): 'The Lord is close to those whose hearts are breaking. . . . The good man does not escape all troubles – he has them too. But the Lord helps him in each and every one. God even protects him from accidents.'

The Lord has shown me that being a Christian does not protect me from pain and suffering. It is part of life and he wants me to know his love in the midst of difficulties. Through human love we have experienced more of God's love. People pray for us, write to us, send cards and books and show genuine concern. If people care this much, how much more must God care.

We have seen that God can use difficulties to do things he could not do otherwise.

He has given us a deeper capacity to understand others who are suffering. He has given Dirk different responsibilities because of his disability, which seem just right for him.

Our own convictions of the Lord have been strengthened. Fears have dominated my mind, fears

Sandra's Perspective (1979)

of the future, fears of dialysis, fears of things that could happen.

It has been a help to me to face these fears and identify them. 'What am I actually afraid of?' Dirk and I have talked them over and in some cases taken definite steps to alleviate them, e.g. taking out life insurance and pursuing buying our own house. Many fears are based on the unknown and the 'what ifs' of life; in these, only trusting God and believing in his sovereignty can help. It helps to find scriptures which apply to the things I'm afraid of.

Psalm 66:8,9 says 'Let everyone bless God and sing his praises, for he holds our lives in his hands, and he holds our feet to the path.' God is holding Dirk's life in his hands — he is sovereign over each of our lives in the family.

The last few years have also held further disappointments which have been tests to our faith and our attitudes.

Dirk was going to have a transplant from his sister, Mary. During the various tests it was discovered that she had kidney stones, which made transplantation impossible.

Our first reaction was 'Why? What is God doing! Does he raise our hopes only to dash them?' We felt rather numb and later very upset. Gradually we came back to the fact that God *is* in control. He knows what is best for Dirk and Mary.

Two years ago we heard of a portable kidney machine which was being developed in Sheffield. We made enquiries and were offered a chance to take it on holiday with us. We planned to go to the Navigator staff conference in Newquay. How excited we were. We practised using the machine in hospital. The results were good. We made preparations to go. The day before we were ready to leave there was a knock on the door. The hospital technicians stood there with long faces – they didn't feel happy for us to take the machine. There were still some problems with the machine that needed to be sorted out.

We felt disappointed and sad. Again we asked, 'What is God doing?' Again we came to the conclusion that God is keeping us from something that may go wrong.

Slowly we learned to thank God in the disappointments because he knows what is best and we are secure in his hands.

People ask us if we have got used to this kind of life. Well! We are more familiar with the procedures, we are used to the routine but dialysis remains just as difficult as ever. It is a constant abnormal procedure which we face three times a week and which saps a considerable amount of emotional energy.

The challenge we face every day is to be able to thank God for that day and for all the good things he has given us and to trust him for daily needs. We do not have the strength to cope in ourselves but he does.

10

Kidney Transplant (1979–80)

'O Love that wilt not let me go'
George Matheson

The phone rang. 'Would you be willing to come into hospital for a possible transplant?' *Would I be willing?* I had been waiting three years for this. Even though I was very willing we were well advised of the risks involved. At that time one-in-ten patients died as a direct or indirect result of transplantation. I remember thinking, 'If this was a game of Russian Roulette would I pull the trigger if there was a one-in-ten chance of getting killed?' I was told that they were unsure whether the kidney was suitable because of possible damage but they weren't able to say at that point. I was too nervous to drive so Sandra took me to the 'Royal' in the city centre. It was one of those old hospitals with incredibly long corridors with huge radiators along the wall. I imagined the cracks in the walls being home to all sorts of germs and bugs. Ominous signs pointed to departments for parts of the body and diseases I had never heard of. Into these departments masked medics disappeared.

I finally found the transplant unit tucked away in a remote corner of the hospital. Transplantation was still in its infancy then.

First of all some tests needed to be done to see if everything was in good order to receive a transplant. One was a check to see if my bladder could cope, not having been used for three years.

Question: 'How can you find out the condition of someone's bladder?' I want to spare you the details but no anaesthetic was used and the test didn't work after various attempts. It still makes me wince, crossing my legs firmly as I think about it!

Finally I was washed and shaved in preparation for the operation and wheeled into theatre awaiting the surgeons who were removing the kidneys from someone who had just died in a car accident. His relatives had given their consent, wanting someone to receive a new life from his tragic death.

I was all ready to be anaesthetised when the doctors came in, still in their theatre gowns. 'We're sorry, but the kidney has been damaged in the accident. We can't take the risk of transplantation.'

So in a daze of unbelief we returned home to once again face the 'Dialysis Régime'. 'Why would God build up my hopes only to dash them again?'

Dialysis became much more difficult to cope with because now my mindset was escape, not endurance. I had glimpsed freedom and was therefore much more dissatisfied with my lot, to say nothing of my

Kidney Transplant (1979–80)

disappointment with God. Every time the phone rang I wondered if it might be the hospital. Every time it rang my spirit would lift for a second only to have it dashed even lower then it was before.

I had to wait another year before *the* phone call came.

One of the major concerns Sandra had was our financial security for the future, or should I say lack of it, especially if something happened to me. She found it very difficult to talk to me about this. Whenever she tried to bring it up I would get angry, not wanting to face the uncertainties of the future.

Just before I had renal failure we had miraculously managed to get a policy on my life which had a decreasing premium culminating in no payout if I died after ten years. We were very grateful for this as most insurance companies wouldn't touch me with a barge pole.

Living in a rented house added to our sense of insecurity. We realised we really needed to be thinking in terms of buying, not only for health reasons but also because we weren't getting any younger.

Having come to the point of recognising the need, we were no further because we didn't have enough savings for a down payment anyway. We had no rich relatives either to hope for a nice inheritance! We considered ourselves to be in God's employ so we decided that the only thing we could do was to ask him about it. The first answer to prayer was when our landlord, who also was a Christian, insisted that we save the rent money instead of giving it to him. Some people heard about our need for a home of our own and incredible as it may sound pledged enough money for us to make a down payment on a house.

We felt it would be better for us to move to Manchester where Sandra's parents and some other close friends lived. We needed to have people around to lend support if needed.

We found a lovely Edwardian house in Didsbury, a pleasant area in south Manchester referred to in the estate agent's brochure as a 'leafy suburb'. The house had a large garden which became a life-saver for me in the years to come. Five bedrooms gave us enough space for a growing family, an office, a room for dialysis and a guest room for our frequent visitors.

The house needed quite a lot of work doing to it. It was while I was over in Manchester that the *call* finally came. Sandra was on the line, barely able to contain her excitement, 'There is a kidney available and they want you to come over right away.'

The Snake Pass as the name implies was not built for speed but I think we set a new speed record crossing the Pennines. I was shaking with a mixture of fear and exhilaration. Whether it was my friend's driving or the anticipation of the transplant I can't say for sure. We headed straight for the Royal Hallamshire Hospital which had a brand new transplant unit on the top floor. This made it easier to protect transplant patients from the possibility of infections. There are marvellous views over Sheffield's Golden Horseshoe – the moorland which surrounds the city on three sides. It was an immaculate building which was opened by the Health Minister saying, 'We don't make them like this any more.' Didn't sound too positive!

I don't remember too much about the actual transplant other than a few kind words from the anaesthetist and an 'Are you awake?' from the nurse after the operation. Nevertheless a new life was beginning for me.

I kept a diary whilst I was in hospital.

Wednesday, 26 March 1980

Each day since the transplant on Saturday night God has given a new victory. Today my hands are free, the drip attached to my arm having been taken out. The catheter was also taken out today after excruciating spasms. Each day I have felt a little better. I don't remember much about Sunday or Monday except being dialysed once. On Tuesday night I thought I was going to die, but Psalm 91 came to mind, 'You will not fear the terror of the night . . . nor the pestilence that stalks in the darkness . . . a thousand may fall at your side . . . but it will not come near you.'

Sandra told me she felt very helped and encouraged. It's strange only being able to talk to her on the internal telephone. (Only medical personnel allowed into the room.) Went for an X-ray.

Thursday, 27 March

Read Psalm 40 today: 'He lifted me out of the slimy pit out of the mud and mire; He set my feet upon a rock and gave me a firm place to stand. . . .

Sacrifice and offering you did not desire, but my ears you have opened.' I felt God saying to me, 'This new life is not so you can make more sacrifices but to *listen* more.'

Not sleeping at night, terrible pain every time I pass urine which is about every 30 minutes. Why all this pain? I never had so much pain and discomfort during dialysis at its worst.

God's timing is so strange. Why build a kidney room in the new house in Manchester? Why transplantation one week before the planned moving date? Why called when in Manchester on first day of week to do some work on the house with friends?

Feel very tense sometimes especially during evenings.

Must remember to be friendly to medical staff and visitors, not live in my own world, be willing to talk, live openly as a Christian.

Friday, 28 March

Rash today, allergic reaction to antibiotic. Slept well for the first time last night.

One of the things I am finding difficult is feeling so dirty and inhuman. I couldn't control my bladder last night so ended up urinating all over my pyjamas. I had to wait 30 minutes to be cleaned up. I smelt awful. I'll be glad when I can have a nice shower.

Saturday, 29 March

am: Slept OK this night — though get very tense about needing to urinate every 20 to 25 minutes. Read about Sarah who laughed at the thought of her body doing something that it had never done before.

Kidney Transplant (1979–80)

'Nothing is impossible for God.' Held onto this verse. It might take a miracle to get my bladder to hold more then the 10 ml it does at the moment. Passing urine is extremely painful though finally my bowels are working normally! I am now able to answer 'Yes' to the question the nurses ask daily. 'Did you open your bowels today?' Another victory, feel better every day. Sandra says many are praying for me and I can believe it.

I find the worst times are in the evening alone and afraid of how things might go at night, but every day God gives me encouragement from what I read in the Bible.

One victory I am grateful for is the removing of some of the connections to my body. The Sunday after the transplant I had a drip in my right arm, dialysis on my left, a catheter in my bladder and two drains from the wound. What a relief when my arm was freed. Today I only have one bottle left to carry around with me!

Stephen is four today, no children allowed in ward.

pm: I am worried about the frequency and pain of the urinating. My bladder holds less now then it did at first. It bothers me most at night because it means severely interrupted sleep.

Sandra said some people are coming around to the house tonight to pray about my bladder function. Is this the first 'bladder' prayer meeting in church history?

Sometimes I ask myself why I need to suffer like this. Job said, 'If he slay me yet will I trust him.' 'Is anything too hard for God?' Must hold onto these verses tonight.

Sunday, 30 March

Had my best night's sleep so far, another victory. Urinating is slightly less painful.

Sandra could come into the room to see me for the first time! Not allowed to touch each other though.

I feel a bit like a caged animal.

My Dad phoned, so did James Fox — this helps: I need the encouragement.

My main desire is that God daily speaks to me and that I truly experience his presence as never before. Reading the stories in Genesis shows me how God picks out ordinary people through whom to show himself. Abraham, Adam and Eve and Noah.

Monday, 31 March

Very good night's sleep and good fellowship with the Lord. Today's victory is more urine produced though blood pressure still too high. Reading *A Step Further* by Joni Eareckson. Excellent! She expresses exactly how I feel. Also read the story of Joseph who after much adversity could say, 'God meant it for good'.

Pete Dowse visited. Visits do encourage me, as do the cards.

Tuesday, 1 April

am: Read Matthew — need to be salt and light in the world but keep my devotional life private.

pm: The kidney doesn't seem to be producing enough urine. There is some fluid retention in my body and I am only passing urine every 45 minutes. Feel worried it might be rejecting.

Jesus was 'sorrowful unto death' and yet he willingly submitted.

I would be terribly sorrowful if Sandra had to have this disappointment and for myself too. 'Please Lord, don't let it fail – encourage me!'

Wednesday, 2 March

First signs of kidney rejection so was given an increased dose of steroids. Still feel well.

Enjoyable visit from Sandra on a beautiful sunny day.

Phone call from Bob Croson; good to speak with him.

Thursday, 3 April

I have been thinking a bit about how I will use my time when I have more. I think God has already said to me that this doesn't necessarily mean more time for activity but more time for listening to him, more time with Sandra, more time with the children.

More signs of rejection which meant needing to go to another hospital for radium treatment. Met Sandra in the corridor as I was being wheeled away. It's her birthday. She was all dressed up, looking great in her red dress, but with tears in her eyes. I'm so sorry this had to happen today!

The doctors don't seem overly concerned about the rejection.

'Please Lord, let there be a significant improvement tomorrow.'

Friday, 4 April, Good Friday

What a difference the crucifixion makes to our lives. How much the world is missing. Listened to and deeply moved by the hymn, 'O love that wilt not let me go'. . .

> O joy that seekest me through pain,
> I cannot close my heart to thee;
> I trace the rainbow through the rain,
> And feel that promise is not vain
> That morn shall tearless be.

Very pleased today with a significant increase in urine output and in a decreasing BP. First signs that the rejection is slowing down.

Had an enjoyable day. Sandra visited. She seemed tired.

Enjoyed reading James Herriot's *Vets Might Fly* today. Very funny, made me laugh out loud.

Saturday, 5 April

Lost weight for the first time but still worried about blood pressure.

Had a nice visit from the children.

Sandra is having a hard time. 'God, will you let me out early so I can help her? Show me what to do.'

Read the Bible but couldn't get into it, felt tired and disturbed. 'Please speak to me Lord.'

I must ask the nurses what they think about Jesus.

Have been in for two weeks now, feeling stronger. Rode two km on the exercise bike. Lost a lot of fluid today and am finally back to my normal weight.

I do pray that Sandra will receive grace for the move and the children.

Sunday, 6 April, Easter

It's a beautiful, sunny day. Missed going to church but read John 9–21.

Sandra came – seemed quite tired. I phoned this evening and she seemed discouraged and daunted by move. Some 'helpers' seem to be getting on her nerves. I wish I was home so I could help. Do I really believe I can help by praying?

Enjoyed reading the *Letters of Samuel Rutherford*. 'Whether God comes to his children with a rod or a crown, if he come himself with it, it is well. Welcome, welcome, Jesus, whatever way you come if we can get a glimpse of you! And sure I am, it is better to be sick, providing Christ come to the bedside and say, "Courage, I am your salvation", than to enjoy good health and never to be visited by God.' Amen to that.

Alan Sims visited, nice to see him.

I feel more and more like going home but praise God, he keeps me happy.

I pray for more opportunities to talk about my faith with the nurses.

Monday, 7 April

Doctors very pleased with results, no more need for any more X-ray treatment. Had the stitches taken out.

Heard that it's not going well with the patient who had a transplant the same time as me. She has a very bad infection, in fact so bad that there is fungal growth in her mouth due to the effect of the immunosuppressants. How awful and scary.

Enjoyed day. Wrote letters and received phone call from Thompy and Gill.

Why has my left leg swollen so much? Looks like an elephant's leg.

Tuesday, 8 April

Leg still very swollen – caused by lymphatic fluid, whatever that is.

A bit bored today. Doctors said I might be able to go home in a few days.

Sandra seemed in good spirits.

Wednesday, 9 April

Had a bit of an argument with Sandra today regarding when to come home. The doctors said possibly Friday – Sandra told the nurses that the house was in a chaotic state and objected to me coming home.

She is under so much pressure especially about the move to Manchester. How I wish and pray that I will be able to help her – she left quite upset. The carpets are being taken up today and the house is in a mess. I'll be glad when we are moved.

Blood pressure still high and leg swollen – not as bad as Margaret in the next room. They have had to stop the steroids to help her recover from an infection, risking the loss of the transplant. She could die!

Had opportunity to talk to one of the nurses about my faith after praying about it the other day.

Thursday, 10 April

Had a good day today – Sandra visited twice.

Could have gone home today! Leg still swollen but praying it will go down. BP down and best blood results to date.

Still enjoying fellowship with the Lord. Noticed in my reading the importance of generosity so sent a gift to a fellow staff member in need.

Sandra seemed to have a good day today.

Face started to swell up today! I hope I don't get the 'moonface' so many people on steroids get.

Friday, 11 April

Read I Samuel – stood out that the most important thing for a leader to do is to learn to listen to God.

Felt lonely and bored today, eager to go home. Sandra phoned and was happy so praise the Lord for that.

Blood results good though BP erratic and leg still worryingly swollen.

Heard that Margaret has started to recover – relieved to hear that.

Doctors said that I can go home tomorrow. Yes!!

11

A New Start in Manchester (1980–81)

> 'Heaven above is softer blue'
> *George Wallace Briggs*

I arrived in Manchester after being carted across the Pennines in the back of Pete Dowse's car. Fresh air can feel indescribably fresh after three weeks in hospital. A hymn came to mind:

> Heaven above is softer blue,
> Earth around is sweeter green.
> Something lives in every hue
> Christless eyes have never seen.
> Birds with gladder songs o'erflow,
> Flowers with deeper beauty shine.

Sandra had moved in the previous day and was there to welcome me into our new home, beautifully decorated with the help of many friends.

For me everything was absolutely new and wonderful but for Sandra feelings were very mixed. The move had been very traumatic for her, coming after weeks of intense pressure, not to mention the preceding four years. The decision-making involved in moving was really more than she could cope with. Actually packing everything into the boxes was just too much. Good friends did the packing for her in Sheffield and James and Mary Fox helped at the new house in Manchester. The removal men, who gave the cheapest quote but were really too old for the job, started complaining to Sandra about moving a particularly heavy piece of furniture. The startled men were suddenly faced with a screaming woman! James hurried to the scene explaining to the men that Sandra was somewhat under stress and Mary ushered Sandra into the lounge. After providing her with a cup of tea Mary carried on unpacking boxes with incredible speed and efficiency. All Sandra could do was to sit there quietly crying to herself.

I was warned of the need to keep away from public places because of the danger of picking up an infection. No restaurants, no church, no cinema and I also needed to be careful about receiving visitors. If anyone came we all had to wear paper face masks.

Keeping a germ-free environment in a house with three lively children with their newly found friends wasn't easy. They would often come in the front door with their pals and go out the back to play in our spacious garden, hanging in trees or the climbing frame with scant regard for the 'patient.'

Sometimes if Sandra was out of the room I would sneak down to the cellar to get a hammer and nail to hang up a picture or something. There are always so many things to do after a move.

Visitors were limited but the phone never stopped ringing, people wanting to know how we were getting on. One caller, Charles Clayton, a friend from Loughborough days, told a particularly interesting story.

'I have just returned from the leadership conference you so much wanted to attend. We had a great time but nothing was as exciting as hearing the news of your successful transplant when I got back. You'll never believe what happened! During the conference it was suggested that people might like to get together in twos to pray about something that was on their heart. I looked over to the other side of the room and my eyes met Nabeel Jabbour, who you know from Lebanon days, of course. Without any verbal communication we both felt we ought to pray together for you. This we did, especially encouraged by Jesus' words, "If two of you on earth agree about anything you ask for, it will be done for you by my Father". When I got back to Britain and heard your news I was so pleased.'

We liked our new house but did find it an adjustment living in the big city. We found the streets very dirty and the presence of tramps disconcerting. Both of us expected everything to be plain sailing now that I had the transplant. Indeed, we were very relieved not to have the constant pressure of dialysis with its accompanying restrictions in lifestyle. But the years had taken their toll on our emotional lives. We just weren't getting on. Sandra didn't feel I was giving her the love, affection and attention she wanted and for that matter I wasn't finding Sandra that easy to relate to either. There were never any major blow-ups but lots of minor irritations. It was all very hard to understand what was going on. On the one hand so happy and on the other very dissatisfied with each other.

I came across an article in *Reader's Digest* called 'Five Myths that Wreck a Marriage' that gave me more understanding. One of the 'myths' was that 'Hard times bring marriage partners closer together'. Statistics showed that couples that faced serious health problems were twice as likely to divorce as those that didn't. As we evaluated our experiences we noticed that so much energy went into coping, just keeping oneself together that there was actually very little left to give to each other. It was something akin to two people who are up to their necks in water and afraid of drowning. Staying alive takes all the energy. Superficially of course what people saw was two people totally involved with one another, but inside it was a different matter. We also noticed that suffering causes a sense of bereavement, bereft of love, so the partner is expected to meet this need but is unable to do so because all the reserves are used up just coping with oneself. The ideal of 'being there' for one another just didn't work. Anger too, seemed to have something to do with it. Perhaps it was an anger about the circumstances that directed itself at the person one was closest to. For Sandra, one of the major considerations was that she had so unselfishly given herself that eventually she had nothing left to give. We gradually began to pick up the pieces to try to rebuild our relationship. We tried to spend more time doing things we enjoyed and listening and talking to one another.

The one to settle into the city most quickly was six-year-old Mark. When asked how he felt about Manchester he said, 'It's the best place on earth'. One of the reasons he probably felt this way was because of his beloved Manchester United. He even had the unique privilege of actually going into the players' dressing room and meeting some of his heroes, like striker Joe Jordan and goalkeeper Gary Bailey. He had his photograph taken with the all-time great Denis Law too.

Mandy, ten years old now, very much missed her good friends from Sheffield and the open-plan school she had attended there. She found Beaver Road School with its more formal atmosphere difficult at first. One of her first observations was that the children were more grown up but not so happy. She felt they considered her childish because she still liked to play with dolls.

Four-year-old Stephen was unsettled by the move but soon began enjoying playschool and loved playing in the garden. He enjoyed being with his little friends but was also quite content on his own.

During this time we kept our friends and financial supporters up to date with regular newsletters. In October 1980 we wrote:

The doctors are very pleased with how everything is going with my kidney. My blood pressure has come down though it does need to come down a bit more. I had my first infections since the transplant a few weeks ago. Steroids lower my resistance to infection and make it harder to overcome them. The infection I had hit me harder then any I can remember. I'm fine now but it did remind us of the dangers we still face. As long as I have the kidney I need the steroids to keep it from rejecting.

We had a very enjoyable summer. We had a week's holiday in the Lake District which was probably one of the best family holidays we ever had. The children were especially happy and contented. We stayed on a farm which had a very playful puppy and kitten which delighted everyone. It was great to be free of all the fuss and bother of my diet. We also went to Holland for two weeks to be with my parents. The children appreciated being with their *Oma* and *Opa* and seeing their aunts, uncles and cousins as well. We all enjoyed the nice Dutch food. Mandy, Mark and Stephen especially liked the variety of spreads for bread – their favourite being hazelnut. The chocolate milk went down a treat as well. As we look back we feel that the relationships in the family have been strengthened.

We had also hoped that the time would be refreshing in our relationship with the Lord but I can't say this was the case. I find that when I am out of active ministry I don't seem to be as stimulated in my devotional life. Perhaps this will improve as I gradually become more involved with people.

After writing this letter my body began to reject the transplanted kidney so I needed to go into hospital for treatment. The doctors gave me a hugely increased dose of steroids to try to stop the rejection. The rejection was arrested but my kidney was damaged causing a reduced function. I found it very difficult to cope with this setback. My expectations of a trouble-free transplant were shattered. My blood pressure had gone up and was not responding to treatment.

Our next letter was sent out in December; this time Sandra wrote:

> This year has been very much a time of adjustments; new house, new school for the children, new neighbours, new church. At first we felt like plants which had been uprooted but now we are beginning to take root again. I can be thankful for our lovely home, for good friends, for being close to my parents, for feeling part of the local church.
>
> When I first came to Manchester I was so tired and emotionally worn out that I found it hard to be positive about anything, even Dirk's transplant wasn't fully appreciated. How faithful God is in loving us and accepting us, providing the right kind of encouragement from others to build us up.
>
> Moving for Mandy has meant leaving old friends and making new ones, leaving a school she loved to a school she is getting to appreciate more and more. It has meant being able to have a room of her own, which she likes very much, having a chance to join a gym club and being able to change from violin to viola. Every move has its

positives and negatives. Mandy still misses her dear friend Rebecca from Sheffield but they still keep in touch and visit one another in the holidays. We are praying that Mandy will find a good friend in Manchester.

Mark has taken to Manchester like a duck to water. He loves playing football with his friends down the road. He is happier at school than he has ever been and is making good progress. We are glad to see he is broadening his interests to include Cricket and Rugby and he has also started playing the clarinet. We are thankful for his contented and happy spirit.

Stephen was rather insecure when we first moved but he has now settled very well. He loves playschool and has made good friends. He has his own individual character in that he seems quite creative, is not keen on football, enjoys playing with Lego and his own cars (not Mark's), listens to stories, and is learning to write. He is eager to start school after Christmas.

In May 1981 I wrote again:

> You may be surprised to know that I have just come out of hospital after having an operation to remove my own kidneys. The doctors felt they might be causing my blood pressure to remain high. The transplanted kidney is still functioning reasonably well though the rejection I had in October has done some damage to the kidney function. In case you are confused by references to no fewer then three kidneys, let me explain!

The transplanted kidney was placed in the front of my body whilst my own kidneys were left intact. Since the operation my blood pressure is still high, however I am taking fewer drugs so there is some progress. I feel better without the unpleasant side-effects of the drugs like headache and depression. When the doctor told me that I had to go into hospital for at least ten days I was a bit upset. You see, I'm not overly fond of hospitals! I felt I needed to get my thoughts and feelings sorted out so I set aside some time to pray and read the Bible. Imagine my encouragement and amusement when the first thing I read was: 'Do not be afraid of what you are about to suffer. I tell you the devil will put some of you in prison to test you and you will suffer persecution for ten days . . .'

Even though the verse talked about being in prison and not in hospital, there probably are some parallels. We all have our own little cells, sometimes unavoidably needing to share with someone we don't like. Surely the food brought to us couldn't be much better than Strangeways. A various assortment of people come around to prod and poke and speak a few words of encouragement to the 'inmate'. When I was in hospital I often thought of this verse and had to chuckle to myself.

On the other hand the phrase 'Do not be afraid of what you are about to suffer' was a real source of encouragement. Fears seem to be magnified especially when lying awake at night. Often I found it helpful to repeat this and other phrases from the Bible to calm my heart and mind.

I was glad to be out after exactly ten days!

One of the things that has clarified recently is the need to go back to review and apply the lessons of the past years on dialysis, i.e.

– the need to focus our minds on God's love and wisdom
– living one day at a time and enjoying whatever He gives
– being thankful
– drawing on God's resources.

When I was on dialysis we felt that one day a transplant would come along and our troubles would be over. Well a transplant came but there were new difficulties and new fears to face. We kept focusing our prayers on the removal of these difficulties rather then accepting them and drawing on God's grace. This in turn brought instability in our emotional and spiritual lives.

Another lesson clarified recently is that when we suffer it takes something out of us, we are weakened, usually feeling more vulnerable. 1 Peter 5:10 promises: 'The God of all grace . . . after you have suffered a little while will himself restore you, make you strong, firm and steadfast.'

In July I wrote again:

We ended our last letter quoting 1 Peter 5: 10. Please continue to pray for us as we don't feel particularly 'strong, firm and steadfast' yet.

The reason we feel this way is that these last months have been especially hard. I've been in hospital for two periods to try to regulate my blood pressure, the kidney is showing signs of deterioration and high blood pressure is causing some unpleasant symptoms. I have had to pull out of a conference that I was planning because the doctors want me back in hospital again.

What in fact has happened is that the kidney was permanently damaged through the rejection I had in the autumn of last year. The kidney is now operating at approximately forty percent of its normal function. This is adequate, but I don't have the strength I had at first and I have some new restrictions in diet. We believe that God has heard our prayers and the prayers of many and is keeping the kidney going. I find it hard to say what we are learning through these experiences, but I think it is primarily the need to focus our minds on and trust in God. Isaiah 64:3,4 has been a real help to us. 'For when you did awesome things we did not expect . . . Since ancient times no one has heard, no ear perceived, no eye has seen any God besides you who acts on behalf of those who wait for him.'

I remember reading this verse the day before the transplant. He certainly did something we didn't expect! We didn't expect to wait so long to see the blood pressure come down either and this verse helps us to keep waiting on God to answer our prayers.

Being out of an active ministry situation has been hard as well. This has caused me to feel quite useless and a failure which in turn leads to discouragement.

A New Start in Manchester (1980–81)

As these letters show, blood pressure was a continuing problem so powerful drugs had to be used to give good control. For a year I had been on a drug that caused depression and some sexual impotence. It wasn't that bad, but I did go to bed mildly depressed each evening. Every time I went to the hospital for a check-up I tried to get them to change the drugs but the considered opinion was that it was better to be mildly depressed and impotent than to risk a heart attack brought on by high blood pressure.

During one hospital visit when I was desperately trying to get out of staying in, one of the doctors I challenged made thing quite clear. 'I am not letting you out of this hospital to have you drop dead on the street.' That shut me up!

Various drug treatments were tried to see which one gave the most effective control of my blood pressure. One of the drugs that helped very much was one called Frusemide. This drug worked by stimulating my body to produce urine. When the urge came I needed to get to a toilet very quickly! I'm sure I set the world 'short-distance-upstairs' record racing to the toilet, especially after a trip in the car.

Regular hospital visits continued with careful monitoring of the kidney function taking place. A pattern began to emerge. The kidney was definitely and steadily deteriorating. 'I believe you are showing chronic rejection symptoms,' the straight-faced doctor said to me, showing no emotion at all. I however, was devastated. So the 'holiday from dialysis' was going to be shorter than expected. So many desires unfulfilled, so many things not done and the feeling that I hadn't used the freedom very well at all.

12

Holiday in America (1982)

'Have patience, don't be in such a hurry'

One of our unfulfilled dreams was to visit America to see my brother Peter and some Navigator friends. We sought some advice about this possibility and, amazingly, as friends heard about it they spontaneously sent money to make the trip possible. But would the doctors let me go? Reluctantly they approved the trip. They were concerned that if I had problems and turned up at an American hospital with unacceptably high levels of impurities in my blood, it could make them look rather irresponsible.

So, flights were booked on the new, cheaper Laker Airways only to have them go bust a few days later! Fortunately, the travel agent hadn't actually transferred our money to Laker so we were able to get a full refund. We felt that God had protected us and we were grateful. We booked this time with Continental Airlines on their 'Fly-Anywhere-in-the USA' tickets.

We packed our bags and set off, full of excitement, down the M6 bound for Heathrow. 'Dad, I think I've forgotten my coat,' piped up Mandy meekly from the back seat. 'Didn't I expressly tell you to check everything before we left,' I replied tersely.

We had just put on a new children's music tape based on the Fruits of the Spirit bought especially for the journey. 'It should help them understand the importance of relating together well.' We had heard songs about love, joy and peace and now came 'patience'.

> Have patience, have patience, don't be in such a hurry.
> Have patience, have patience then you won't need to worry.

Laughter had already begun to mix with the frustration and soon it won the day.

We boarded the Jumbo jet that was to take us to our first stop, Boston. How do they get these flying hotels into the air?

Steve and Cindy Covell, Navigator friends we knew from their time in England, met us at the airport and took us to their spacious home in the suburbs of Washington, DC.

The next day we did a quick tour of the major sights of the Capitol spending most of our time at the Air and Space Museum. Seeing the historic planes made me realise just what a major part America has had in the development of flight. All the significant

Holiday in America (1982)

planes were there, the Kitty Hawk, the Spirit of St Louis, right up to the most recent spacecraft like the Apollo.

I'll never forget *The History of Flight* in the circular cinema, with sound and picture all around us. We all ducked and weaved and sometimes nearly fell over as the camera took us right across America, in a balloon, on a train, in a roller coaster, in a light aircraft and then a low-flying jet. We left the cinema exhilarated and disoriented, walking out into the museum blinking and trying to get our bearings.

We were in America, so on the way home Steve wanted to treat us to some doughnuts – an all-American treat. 'I know where a "Dunkin Donut" place is, it's just around the corner . . . or is it this corner . . . or that corner?' The neighbourhood was becoming more and more rough looking but at last we spotted one. It wasn't the one he was looking for but still, it was a doughnut shop. Steve bravely went ahead and I followed. The people in the shop looked up at us unsmilingly. We felt conspicuously 'white'. We ordered our doughnuts, paid the money and ran . . . No we didn't. We tried to show no fear and casually returned to the car. The fact that Steve was an ex-army man and had actually stood guard at John F. Kennedy's grave was no comfort to me at all. The doughnuts were terrific though!

We flew from Boston right across America to Los Angeles. I was staggered at the vastness of America. It's very easy as a European to underestimate its power and influence.

My brother and his wife welcomed us with typical American generosity. They even moved out of their own home so that we would have somewhere nice to stay. Our children loved my brother's den and went into it at about 5:00 am every morning to watch cartoons. My brother made his T-Bird available to us as well. An opportunity to experience my teenage dream.

Seven days to do Los Angeles – eat out as often and as much as possible. How do you cope when a sign offers, 'All you can eat for $5.00'? Eat until you feel sick – that's what.

Disneyland, Universal Studios, Knott's Berry Farm. Where do you start? Well, Disneyland, that's where! Frontier Land, Adventure Land, Tomorrow Land, get your picture taken with Mickey Mouse, walk along immaculate boulevards. I had never seen cleaner streets, not even in Holland. Attendants in bright white uniforms pick up every scrap of paper and every cigarette butt with a handy custom-made implement.

So many places to eat. Many queues. Some an hour long, the lines on the pavement confirming your estimated waiting time. It was worth the one-hour wait for Space Mountain. This is a huge globe-shaped building housing an indoor roller coaster. Sailing through the darkness with incredible special effects makes you feel as if you really are in space, weightless.

When Mark was a little lad I took him to the Blackpool Pleasure Beach and bribed him to go on the more scary rides with me, but no bribes were needed here. 'Can we do it again, Dad?' Later, 'Let's go to the haunted house next.'

We've all been on spooky rides — so called with the totally predictable mechanical skeletons popping up — all right for making little girls scream but not grown up men like me, but this was different.

We all went into a room in which the floor suddenly seemed to fall away as if we were descending to a great depth. At the same time the faces on the portraits on the walls of the room began to age alarmingly. A door opened and we were all directed into cars which took us through the darkness with various spooks and the like popping up. We passed a large saloon-style ballroom with transparent figures dancing in the dim light. On reflection it was obviously done with cameras but coming across it for the first time I didn't know what to make of it, it was so lifelike. On the way out Stephen and I could see our reflection in the mirror but I could have sworn there was a ghoul sitting on our shoulders. Great fun!

No one leaves Disneyland without a soft cuddly toy. We bought Mandy a Dumbo, Mark a Mickey Mouse and Stephen a Goofy.

Next stop Universal Studios. We didn't know what to expect here. Was it just an enormous boring studio? Far from it.

No sooner had we boarded a train to take us around the studio, when we heard the sound of a huge locomotive bearing down on us, only to have it stop a split second before it would have hit us. Next, we drove over a bridge which collapsed as we went over, running straight into a lake that miraculously parted before us, just like the Red Sea did for Moses in *The Ten Commandments*. We passed through a wall of water. Coming up out of the water we were ready for a nice tranquil ride beside the lake only to find 'Jaws' leaping out of the water to within inches of our faces. Screams and laughter. 'Let's do it again, this is great!'

The train then passed through an amazing revolving ice tunnel and on into a Star Wars set with lasers blazing.

Finally we went into the actual studio to see even more special effects. Volunteers were asked for on the set of Superman. Feeling that my big break had finally come I dragged Sandra with me onto the stage. She was to be my Lois Lane. The children watched aghast. This wasn't the kind of thing their boring old Dad did! I had to put on an old moth-eaten Superman outfit and lie on a small platform in a traditional Superman flying pose. It didn't look like much to me but those who could see the screen behind me could see that Superman, alias Dirk van Zuylen, was flying admired by his beautiful assistant Lois (Sandra) Lane.

Next stop Knott's Berry Farm. Who is Knott's Berry you may ask. Well it's Knott's *Berry* of Boysenberry fame. (For the horticulturist, it's a cross between a youngberry and a loganberry and makes wonderful jam.) Once again there were wonderful whiteknuckle rides and entertaining shows. On the way around the park we were held up by gun-toting but friendly cowboys. We were on our way to

Holiday in America (1982)

Montezuma's Revenge, the ride that finally gave me irrefutable evidence that I was no longer a teenager. Only Mandy was willing to go on it with me. Basically the ride is a simple loop with a vertical rise on either side – no problem! What I didn't expect was that as the car got to the top of the loop it nearly came to a stop and did so again at the other end of the ride virtually suspending us in mid-air. I gave Sandra a feeble wave and smile down below when it went the same route again but this time going backwards. Mandy seemed fine but I really felt sick, my head aching. 'Are you all right?' Sandra enquired. 'Yes, I'm fine,' I said as I weaved my way towards the exit. Montezuma had extracted his revenge on the white man.

One of the good things about my brother's house in Pacific Palisades (where Ronald Reagan lived we were told) was that we were very close to the beach. What fun it was to sit on the beach in a bathing costume in March.

We also travelled North to Visalia to visit our old friends from Manchester days, Gordy and Margaret Nordstrom. The mountains we drove through were quite spectacular and it was fun driving the Ford Thunderbird. The only frustrating thing about it was the 50 mph speed limit. What's the point of having such a powerful engine if you can't demonstrate its power?

After a great time with them we returned to Los Angeles and flew on to Portland, Oregon via Denver, Colorado. Not the most obvious route you might say.

Our Continental Airways ticket meant that we needed to use their flight paths and there wasn't a direct link to Portland from LA. For good measure Stephen was sick because of the turbulence going over the Rockies.

Anyway, we finally arrived somewhat tired in Portland to be welcomed by the Brase family, with whom I had lived in Holland.

After a good night's sleep at their house in Beaverton we were asked if we fancied going 'tubing' that day. 'Tubing? What's that?' 'It's a big inflatable tube with handles that's used to slide down a hill,' Lee said. 'We're all for that.' So off we set up to Mount Hood, getting a view of the steaming Mount St. Helens on the way.

Sandra wasn't too keen on tubing but when she saw Lee's mother, who was in her seventies, eager to go down she felt she had to try it too. Screeching with excitement, colliding, and sometimes falling off we slid down the hillside.

Lee and Marilyn lived outside the city with their daughter and three boys. Basketball, baseball, football and soccer. Mark was in his element with the boys but like all good things it comes to an end and it was time to go. 'I am not coming,' said Mark in no uncertain terms. 'What do you mean you're not coming, we have to leave now.' 'No! I am not coming.' This was the first full-scale rebellion we ever had to face from Mark. Anyway, with much persuasion, pleading and threatening he finally came with us. It's a good thing he did or else he would have missed the next exciting adventure.

Holiday in America (1982)

Fond farewells were said and it was off to Colorado Springs and Glen Eyrie, the International Headquarters of the Navigators. Glen Eyrie is a unique castle in America as it was built in true Scottish style with material brought over by the first owner from his home country. It is set in the foothills of the majestic Rocky Mountains surrounded by magnificent stone features appropriately called the 'Garden of the Gods'.

We were treated like honoured guests and were given a large family room in the castle to stay in. We were very grateful to be given so many wonderful experiences but I often felt guilty. Sometimes I didn't feel worthy or that it was right for a Christian worker to have so much fun!

It was while staying in that lovely bedroom overlooking the beautiful snow-covered Rockies that I read some verses in Ecclesiastes. Here is what I read: 'Moreover when God gives a man possessions and enables him to enjoy them . . . this is a gift of God.'

'And enjoy life with the wife whom you love.'

These verses helped confirm to me that it was all right to enjoy the things being given to us. Perhaps it's a Puritan streak in me that says enjoyment must be wrong. Anyway, 'Thanks God, point taken'.

The next day we went to the Flying W ranch for a Cowboy Evening with real gunfighters. When it comes to entertainment, no one can put on a show like the Americans. An extravagant meal of huge steaks for us with mountains of salad and enormous plate-sized hamburgers for the children was somehow consumed. Gunfighters and quick-draw artists did their stuff delighting us all and mixing with the customers afterwards.

Part of the American Western experience is horseback riding so off we went to a 'Dude Ranch'. Jack Palance wasn't there but this wasn't the only disappointment. The horses appeared to be computer programmed to go at an incredibly docile pace. It didn't matter how much bouncing up and down in the saddle we did or clicks or 'giddy ups' nothing speeded those horses up. Even Mandy who knew how to ride couldn't get her horse to go any faster. It didn't matter though, we were all having such fun but the time was fast approaching to go home.

We had one further incident on the way back. Stephen had bought a very realistic-looking toy Frontier rifle at Disneyland that he was very fond of but the aeroplane regulations are quite clear. 'No guns, including toys ones are allowed on the plane.' It was too long to hide it in the suitcase so we had to declare it. We felt that it wasn't appropriate to enter into a discussion about 'our inalienable right to bear arms'. 'We'll see what we can do,' they said at the check-in desk. Finally it was arranged that the toy gun could be kept in the pilot's cockpit. Stephen was thrilled and it was another sign to us of God's goodness to us on this trip. We arrived back in England full of memories and photographs to discover an even greater sign of God's goodness. The next hospital visit showed that there had been no further deterioration of the kidney. The final fling wasn't what we had anticipated it to be as the kidney function actually improved over the next few months.

Holiday in America (1982)

I felt a bit of a fraud having told people that the days of the transplanted kidney were numbered.

I was glad to be back in Britain. As I reflected on our time in America I realised that even though I was enjoying myself immensely I felt as if something was missing but couldn't put my finger on exactly what it was. It was like a landscape without landmarks. Finally I realised that what it lacked for me was a sense of history. I felt this especially in California. Older buildings give me a sense of perspective. I can't prove this though, perhaps it's just a feeling.

Another reason I was glad to be back was because the time had tapped into some very deep and hidden, painful memories from my youth in Canada. It had something to do with being foreign. It also had something to do with not being especially popular or excelling at anything in particular. As a young person I felt that Canadians related to me the same as to anyone else; that was until I did something wrong. Then I was called a 'stupid Dutchman'. Another feeling that went very deep was the sense that it only matters to win, to be the best. In my school reports I always came out as 'average'. Seeing *Top Gun*, starring Tom Cruise focused it very much for me when he asked what would happen if he gained second place. 'It's all about being Top Gun, the replay came, there is no place for number two.'

I felt that in Europe people were generally more accepting towards each other regardless of achievement. I had many happy memories of growing up in Canada but felt more at home here.

13

Pain and Pleasure (1982–88)

'This Woman's Work'
Kate Bush

The so-called chronic rejection had miraculously stopped. The doctors were very surprised and pleased but couldn't account for the remission. I suggested that it was perhaps an answer to prayer but this seemed to reflect badly on their medical expertise so I didn't press the point. The following years were quite a mixture of pain and pleasure.

The transplant had made me aware of the cost the family paid because of my ill health and I felt I needed to pay more attention to them individually, not only Sandra but the children as well. In fact it was that very phrase 'the children' that I realised needed to disappear from my thinking and vocabulary. They weren't 'the children' they were Mandy, Mark and Stephen. They each had their own distinct personalities

Mandy was now a teenager, full of life, strong-minded, creative and kind. She blazed the trail in 'parental training', shifting us from some of our preconceived ideas and moving us into the real world that adolescents live in today. She was able to articulate clearly and sometimes dispassionately her point of view on matters of importance. Sometimes Mandy and I did get into seriously heated arguments. Our most serious conflict came during the miners' strike a few years later. I was so upset at her apparent lack of appreciation for my point of view I went to bed in a huff at 3:00 in the afternoon to sulk. Sandra wasn't very impressed with her husband and told me in no uncertain terms to act like a father, get out of bed and sort things out. I had to apologise and as usual found Mandy very forgiving, but firm.

Mandy was creative in music and art (winning a prize in a city-wide painting competition). She played the piano and violin. Sport continued to be an interest – especially hockey. Duran Duran (cringe) and Madness were her favourite groups at the time.

Ten-year-old Mark too was into Madness in a big way and could do brilliant imitations of them. Dressed in a black sports jacket, various 'Ska' buttons on each lapel and wearing his granddad's bowler hat (left over from his grandfather's employer's, 'Nice one, Cyril' campaign), he would do a jerky, stooping strut, arms swinging and sing, 'Baggy Trousers'.

> Naughty boys in nasty schools,
> Headmasters breaking all the rules . . .
> Oh what fun we had
> but at the time it seemed so bad . . .

> Baggy trousers, dirty shirts,
> pulling hair and eating dirt . . .

Madness were appearing at the Apollo in Manchester and I was pleaded with and harassed into buying tickets. I bought these tickets with rather mixed motives, thinking that it would be good to do something with them but at the same time it would be a good object-lesson as to what good, Christian children shouldn't be interested in. I expected the concert to be 'worldly' and that it would be obvious to them that it wasn't appropriate entertainment for them. The long-awaited concert finally arrived and off we went, the three of us.

As soon as Madness came onto the stage everyone got on their feet. I didn't remember people doing that at the Peter, Paul and Mary concert I went to 16 years earlier! Everyone started jumping up and down to the music and waving their arms in the air. 'Hey, these guys are good.' I entered into the 'gig' (new word in my vocabulary) more and more. On the way home we were all singing 'Baggy Trousers'. I was trying to 'convert' them but in fact old Dad got converted!

Besides being keen on Ska music Mark remained a devoted fan of Man. United. He informed me casually that he was better than me at football and I had to agree. A friend of mine offered him a fiver if he could keep the ball in the air a hundred times without it touching the ground and after much practice he did actually manage it.

Pain and Pleasure (1982–88)

Mark was a fun-loving lad who was never short of friends. He was always out, coming back only to sleep and eat.

School was a different matter. Our local school was very supportive of academic achievers and musicians, but for lively 'lads' like Mark there was little tolerance. At this time he began to feel that he was perhaps a 'thicky', which he certainly wasn't, and already began to despair of ever getting a job. One teacher described Mark as 'always on the edge of trouble'. He wasn't a troublemaker but he always liked to be where the action was. His last teacher at Junior School resigned at the end of his year. The fact that she picked up an ink-filled plasticine ball from Mark's desk and got it all over her dress had nothing to do with it!

Space Invaders were all the rage with Mark, as with many children at that time. Bleep, bleep, bleep, bleep, bleep, crash, bleep, bleep, bleep, bleep, bleep, bleep. 'Go and play somewhere else with that **** thing.'

Stephen who had been born under traumatic circumstances was a cheerful, sensitive and conscientious seven-year-old. He enjoyed Beaver Road School where he had a few good friends. He, like Mandy, was interested in art and music and was given the opportunity to sing in the Manchester Boys' Choir. Even though there was a gruelling practice schedule he really enjoyed it. Stephen also had piano lessons and learnt to play the flute. Not content with artistic pursuits alone he liked to play cricket and rugby too.

Because of the relative stability of my health I was able to get more stuck into my work which I liked very much. I was involved mainly in the development of Navigator staff members in the North of England and Scotland, about eight people in all. I was also a member of the national leadership body of our work. It was very satisfying for me to visit the student groups. I would spend time talking to the group leaders and also with the young students talking with them about their faith. I was especially pleased when opportunities came my way to introduce the Christian faith to people.

My energy was limited due to my low haemoglobin so I had to manage my time very well. Migraines, which I hadn't had since being on dialysis, started again causing me too be very sick from time to time. One time I just wasn't able to keep anything down so the doctor ordered an ambulance to take me to the hospital. If I wasn't sick before I started that journey being thrown back and forth in the back of the ambulance made sure that all reasonable doubt of the need for hospitalisation was removed by the time I arrived. After administering some fluid directly into my system I soon recovered.

We had moved to Manchester from Sheffield because we felt that we needed supportive relationships. Soon after we arrived our good friends and colleagues Gordy and Margaret Nordstrom returned to America. On July 15 1982 Sandra's father died suddenly of a heart attack whilst out on a bowling green. We missed him very much. He was a kindly man who had suffered greatly in the Second World War having been taken prisoner upon arrival in Singapore. He was put to work on the notorious

Pain and Pleasure (1982–88)   141

Burma railway but never showed any bitterness towards his persecutors. Whenever he saw me he would always ask how I was and if I said, 'I'm well, thanks,' he seemed genuinely pleased. He had an ability to enjoy life which he passed onto his daughter, for which I am truly grateful.

We had to take on a more caring role towards Sandra's mother who missed 'Jack' terribly. 'I lost a pal,' she said.

In the autumn of 1984 Sandra started a part-time job at the cytology lab at Christie's Hospital, which wasn't far from where we lived. She found this quite challenging but enjoyed the opportunity to get out into the 'big wide world' now that there were no small children at home during the day.

Because I was free of dialysis I was able to travel more. In 1986 I was invited to go to Finland to speak at some conferences. I visited three times, once just near Christmas. How enchanting it was to see bright lights in the windows of the houses in a land shrouded in winter darkness from mid-afternoon. Since my visit, we too display a candelabra with seven lights. Another custom I liked was the placing of large candles out of doors to welcome guests as they arrive in mid-winter.

I really appreciated the gentle warmth of the Finns which seemed to me more like the warmth of a stove than a blazing fire.

I took to saunas like a duck to water. In Britain I had a go once or twice but never saw the point of sitting in a claustrophobic shed, sweating like a pig and then punishing yourself further by jumping into a cold bath!

In Finland it all seemed to be more natural – or should I say *au naturel*! My first experience of a Finnish sauna was in their glorious countryside. A land of sparklingly clear lakes and literally thousands of islands (one for each person in the country presumably).

I was speaking at the conference in the morning and in the afternoon I was invited to join the men for the sauna. (Men and women separate, this was a Christian conference!) I was a bit reluctant because of my previous experiences but was keen to sample the culture. There was a terrific atmosphere, lots of laughs and if you like a bit of sadism you can beat yourself with some branches. After some time, ten minutes for beginners like me, it was time to race to the cool lake and jump in. This was the most enjoyable part for me. The cool water felt so good on my hot body. By the way, the semi-nude sprint to the lake is done in summer and winter! I repeated this process a few times before sitting outdoors for the final cooling off period. Actually the best part was getting into bed at night. My skin felt so clean and glowing and I slept like a log.

As a thank-you gift for my work there I received a collection of Sibelius' works and some exquisite Finnish glass for which they are justly famous.

Because the transplant had now lasted for six years I was feeling more confident about my future, but was suddenly brought down with a bump. My kidney showed a sudden deterioration. The cause for this was that through some mix-up with my prescription I was taking too low a dosage of steroids. For about eight weeks I had been on too low a dose without realising it. I was now operating on about a 20% kidney function and my haemoglobin was consequently quite low. This meant feeling quite out of breath. One person commented after hearing me speak, 'I have never heard anyone pant so much giving a talk.'

The possibility for me to be placed back on the transplant list was discussed, believing that the kidney wouldn't last much longer. I was very relieved when a few months later things stabilised and so I didn't need to go back on the transplant list. It was quite a disturbing time because it had put us back in touch with the suppressed feelings about dialysis.

I think that the difficulties were actually affecting me more than I realised, making it harder to cope with the normal ups and downs of family life. We enjoyed our children most of the time but there was plenty of conflict between siblings. Sometimes they weren't very nice to me either! One time on holiday I got so fed up I left home! Seeing as I wasn't appreciated I felt that I might as well leave. I walked into the nearest village planning how I was going to proceed from there and thinking about how I was going to inform them of my departure. 'Once I'm gone they'll appreciate me and regret being so nasty to me.' After some careful thought it all seemed a bit silly so I returned to the holiday cottage. No one had even noticed my absence!

I received blood transfusions from time to time. These gave me sudden bursts of energy but this only lasted for a few weeks. It was more frustrating in the end because it focused my mind on what might be rather than living a life that was appropriate to my circumstances. The weakness also meant I had to cut down on my workload which led to me feeling useless which in turn made me feel depressed. To a great extent, my work is my life. The pattern I noticed was that if I worked, I was affirmed by people and therefore motivated to give more. Conversely, if I did less, the lack of affirmation confirmed my sense of not being very useful. These feelings would cause me to withdraw even more and this of course led to a greater sense of uselessness. I told myself that this new sense of worthlessness was justifiable because I probably had been fooling myself with an inflated sense of my own importance anyway! Sometimes I felt that my whole life was a charade and now at last I was being exposed and deservedly so. It felt like looking into a deep dark pit and it was very frightening.

Nevertheless I still was able to respond in May 1987 to an invitation from a friend and colleague, James Broad, to go to Australia to visit the Navigator work there.

What an amazing country it is! No wonder it has become so popular over the last few years, partially due I'm sure to the added publicity given by *Neighbours* and *Crocodile Dundee*. James and I very much enjoyed meeting the people. They were so generous and spontaneous, exuding confidence. I felt very much at home there. One reason may have been that they seemed to me to be North American in their manner but British on the inside. It struck me that their self-deprecating humour and way of thinking was much like many British people I know, yet their outgoing nature and love of sport reminded me of the people I had grown up with in Canada.

We enjoyed a visit to Melbourne, Victoria. Indeed, there were Victorian buildings in the city but the many modern buildings gave a very forward-looking feel to the place. The highlight of our time was a visit to the Art Gallery, where we were introduced to Australia's own artistic heritage, that we in the West are largely ignorant of, or at least I was. The paintings give a sense of Australia's own unique history. One, called *The Pioneer* by Frederick McCubbin painted in 1904 describes their development very movingly. The very large picture is divided into three panels, the central, larger one depicting a settler sitting on a tree he had just felled and talking to his wife, who is holding a baby. Their newly built log cabin is in the background. The first panel shows them just having arrived in the 'bush' with the settler's wife sitting wistfully in the foreground as he tends a fire. The final panel shows a modern Australian discovering an old wooden grave marked with a simple cross. A city can be seen in the distance. It has to be said that the initial impact of this outstanding picture is marred by the myriad cheap reproductions that are on sale seemingly everywhere. Perhaps this is one of the downsides of their enterprising culture!

My favourite picture in the gallery is *The Lesson* by E. Phillips which is in the same Australian Impressionist style. It is a charming picture simply portraying a woman and a little girl reading a book together.

After the time in Melbourne I had the opportunity to take a bus cross-country to Sydney which enabled me to view the varied landscape. The scenery was so different from anything I had seen in the previous places I had lived. The eucalyptus trees make an immediate impact with their light, peeling bark and unusual grey foliage. The landscape is frequently quite barren with occasional sparsely populated settlements that often have aboriginal names. Names like Wagga Wagga, Cootamundra and Mount Bogong give a very strong sense of other-worldliness.

The first thing that struck me on arriving in Sydney was the houses. So many beautiful, detached houses with swimming pools in the garden. The suburbs seemed to go on forever. Entering the city, the scale and robustness of the buildings impressed me. The harbour with its stunning Opera House is surely one of the most beautiful in the world! All this is enhanced by a very balmy climate.

We had the opportunity to go out into the harbour as our host actually owned a small boat. This gave an even better opportunity to see the famed Opera House. It was great fun steering the boat myself for a while. There must be some salt in my veins!

P.S. We also did some work there, speaking at conferences and advising the Australian staff members.

Pain and Pleasure (1982–88)

James and I returned home via Singapore (what an airport!) and Bahrain (brought back memories of my days in Beirut). Our time clocks were all out of order and we found ourselves drinking beer (non-alcoholic, honest!) at 7:00 am GMT.

I was so enthusiastic about Australia when I got back that Sandra was afraid I might emigrate, with or without her.

Seven months later a new and different pain was to be faced.

Sandra wrote to our friends:

On the 23rd of February my mother went to be with the Lord.

The last few weeks have been a combination of great joy and great pain.

Mum went into hospital mid-December and was operated on for a large swelling in her abdomen. It was discovered that she had cancer affecting her liver, and nothing could be done. The doctors did not expect her to make a full recovery from the operation but thankfully she did, and came to live with us on January 1st. I gave up my job at the lab to look after her.

Although she was very sick, her attitude and love have been an example to our family and all her friends. She accepted the situation very positively and made the best of each day. Our relationship has been wonderful over these weeks, our love has deepened and we had many precious times together. She made every effort right up to the last week of her life to get up, and wash and dress herself.

> The last week was very distressing seeing her deteriorate daily. We had a beautiful last communion service conducted by her vicar. Afterwards she peacefully told me that she was putting her hand into Jesus' hand. A few days later she died peacefully.
>
> We are very grateful to God for these precious weeks with her and the strength he gave to cope right up to the end. We are once again aware that, 'his strength is made perfect in weakness'.

My relationship with Sandra's mother had never been an easy one. Deep down I suppose I didn't feel approved of. Nothing was ever said, there were no arguments or heated exchanges.

Certain experiences seemed to give focus to these feelings. I don't think I gave the impression that I was a man who could give her daughter financial security because I had no fixed wage – living on 'charity' as it was called. Taking Sandra off to Holland probably didn't help either.

Sandra's parents did come to visit us in Holland but I'm not sure what kind of impression I gave as a father either. We were once out in a park with Mandy in her carrycot when I picked it up and accidentally let go of one of the handles. The cot turned over on its side and out rolled one-month-old Mandy onto the grass. I can still see it now, as if in slow motion. The only harm that was done was to my pride, Mandy hardly noticed.

Another memory is of planting a considerable amount of crocuses that my father had given me in her garden. When they came up the following spring her only comment to me was, 'He gave me all the blue ones!' (Mine were white, which perhaps she preferred.) I was more than a little peeved at this remark and Sandra's assurance that this was the 'Northern way' and that I wasn't to take it too seriously didn't help. I needed to learn that giving should be a genuine service, not to solicit appreciation but simply to express love.

The time that Sandra's mother stayed with us was very healing for me. It helped me to see that though Manchester people can seem unaffectionate or inexpressive of intimate feelings it doesn't mean that these feelings are absent. On the contrary, I experienced real warmth and affection from her towards me and to all the family in those days.

We had rearranged our lounge for her and placed a large leather recliner in the corner of the room for her to sit comfortably or sleep if she wished. We all gave her plenty of attention and she graciously received it. Even though she was often in pain she spread sunshine in that room. Our teenagers would come in after school and have a chat with her. She would give them chocolate or whatever was to hand. (With Mark this was done surreptitiously as he wasn't really allowed sweets.)

The pain increased as she neared the end of her life and she was eventually confined to bed. Our own bed was especially comfortable so Sandra and I moved into the spare bedroom. Our pain too increased as we watched her suffer – it was just too hard to watch.

Towards the end we prayed that God would take her. We were so grateful that we could share these last precious days with her.

Meanwhile my blood tests showed a steady deterioration that year and dialysis began to loom on the horizon. I was transferred to the 'pre-dialysis' clinic also known as the 'End Stage Renal Failure' clinic. Neither name appealed to me. I didn't like the sound of either of them.

Gradually I was feeling worse and was ill more frequently. I wasn't well enough to take Mandy to Newcastle University to start her course in English literature so my friend Ron Finlay kindly drove her there.

Memories came flooding back, the needles, the diet, the restless sleep, the nausea. I was sitting in our lounge, the room beautifully and creatively decorated for Christmas by Sandra, Mandy's new CD was playing in the background and I began to cry, weeping quietly to myself thinking, 'I just can't face it again'. Mandy happened to come into the room and put her arms around me, weeping with me and comforting me as only a daughter can. She expressed her concern for me, but years later she told me just how devastating it was for her to see her father broken down.

The music suddenly drifted into my consciousness. Kate Bush was singing, 'This Woman's Work'.

Pray God you can cope . . .
Ooh it's hard on the man . . .

Pain and Pleasure (1982–88)

I know you have a little life in you
I know you have a lot of strength left . . .
I should be crying but I just can't let it show,
I should be hoping but I can't stop thinking
Of all the things I should've said, that I never said,
All the things we should have done, that we never did,
All the things I should've given but I didn't.
Oh, darling make it go, make it go away.

How would Sandra cope? I had brought so much pain into her life already.

14

Renal Failure Again (1989)

'Comfort ye my people'
Handel's Messiah

A few weeks before Christmas I arrived at the clinic to be told that the senior consultant, Dr Gokal, wanted to see me. I had learned that when senior hospital doctors are interested in you it is definitely not a good sign! He informed me that I would soon need to start dialysis and that he had booked me into the Manchester Royal Infirmary to start on 3 January when a bed would be available. His gentle caring manner was assuring but this didn't soften the blow at all. 'What a way to enter 1989,' I thought.

As I was adjusting to the thoughts of dialysis again something else was causing alarm. A few days before I was to start I went to the toilet and was shocked to see the bowl red with blood. I didn't know what to do so I flushed it away immediately, pretending to myself that I had seen nothing. It really turned my stomach and scared me. I didn't want to bring it to Sandra's attention at all. When this happened again the next day I knew something needed to be done and so I told her about it. The next time this happened I took a sample straight to the hospital. The renal doctor, 'Dr Joe', seemed as worried as I was and insisted that I be immediately admitted for tests even though it was New Year's Eve. Later that day, another specialist saw the blood sample, did an internal examination but he wasn't sure of the cause. The sample was disposed of. The next day there was no new loss of blood, another younger doctor did what seemed to me a cursory examination and diagnosed haemorrhoids. 'We'll have you come in at a later date to have them seen to,' he said and sent me home. Two days later I was back to start with dialysis.

The battle between the transplanted kidney and my immune system had finally been won by my own body's 'defence' system I had heard someone describe the body as 'xenophobic' i.e. it always seeks to reject whatever it sees as foreign. Steroids slowed this process down but in the end the antibodies triumphed. It was in fact a miracle that the transplant had lasted as long as it did after the damage done by the rejections in the early days. A rejection basically destroys the cells of the kidney which are not able to rejuvenate. The remaining cells had done the best they could to make up the slack but ultimately they too failed!

I was reminded of the Bible verse Mrs Graeme had sent many years earlier, 'I will restore to you the years which the swarming locust has eaten.' I had been restored by the nine years of the transplant after the four years of dialysis.

I had to relearn the complex working of dialysis and the kidney machine although there had been major improvements in the intervening years. We now had smaller disposable kidneys, though contrary to the makers' instructions we used them more than once. We also had kidney machines that gave a more gentle dialysis through better control of the chemicals used in the process. Another benefit was that I could train as an outpatient rather than needing to be hospitalised. Even better was that they had revised the strategy of waiting until I was at 'death's door' before starting dialysis.

One thing that hadn't changed was the busy-ness of the nursing and technical staff due to inadequate staffing levels. There seemed to be no time for personal attention. The only person who ever expressed any tangible sympathy to me was Hazel, one of the helpers whose job it was to prepare the machines for dialysis. She gently placed her hand on my shoulder as a gesture of sympathy one time when I was feeling particularly unwell after the treatment.

Whilst dialysing, most patients watched television, read or dozed. I knew it would be quite a while before the room in our house would be ready for dialysis so I decided I would take something substantial to read. I borrowed *War and Peace* and actually did finish it though it took me a long time to get into it. It was helpful to have something to focus my mind on for the six hours, three times a week. Sometimes I listened to the radio or to a cassette on my Walkman. I had recently bought tapes by the

Eurythmics and Simple Minds (both Scottish). I especially liked Simple Minds' rendition of 'Belfast Child'.

Because Mandy had started reading English at Newcastle University that Autumn she was able to put me in touch with some excellent books about which we often had stimulating conversations. We subscribed to the *Great Writers Collection* which introduced us to a new classic every two weeks. I started with some early novels like *Jane Eyre* and *Wuthering Heights* which were a joy to read. I loved Jane Austin's use of the English language and insight into human nature. *Tess* by Thomas Hardy provided good material for thought. The twentieth-century writers like James Joyce, E.M. Forster (who was very much in vogue at the time) and D.H. Lawrence I found more thought-provoking. What I found particularly interesting was how in a number of their books there was an underlying theme of what I would call 'liberation through free sex'. I often wondered what they would have made of our society which actually achieved 'free sex'. Mandy recommended reading Virginia Woolf and tried to explain 'stream of consciousness' to me! Probably her *Mrs Dalloway* influenced me more than any other. Basically it's a simple tale about a women preparing to give a party. I felt that what the writer was trying to say to a male-dominated world was that a woman's day, whatever she did, was as valid as any male politician's, soldier's or doctor's day or the ordinary man's for that matter.

And then there is Charles Dickens! Every Christmas I try to read, out loud if possible, *A Christmas Carol* for the pure joy of his exquisite descriptions.

> Scrooge, a squeezing, wrenching, grasping, scraping, clutching, covetous, old sinner! Hard as flint, from which no steel ever struck out generous fire; secret and self-contained, solitary as an oyster. The cold within him froze his old features, nipped his pointed nose, shrivelled his cheek, stiffened his gait; made his eyes red, his thin lips blue . . .

Whilst in hospital I watched daytime television especially when I wasn't feeling too well.

I also became an expert on 'women's issues' by reading the various women's magazines lying around in the hospital.

The old side effects gradually began to return. My joints started to be painful all the time. The itchiness was always such a nuisance. Sandra would have to laugh as she often found me rubbing my back against a door post like Baloo Bear in Disney's *Jungle Book* to reach the inaccessible parts. I also had 'restless legs syndrome' which meant that at night I couldn't rest properly, my legs suddenly kicking out, often at Sandra who was within striking distance. I had no control over this kicking, (honest!). We did however get an extra large bed to prevent any further wife abuse.

I couldn't settle down to sleep at night even after taking two or three sleeping tablets. It was usually two or three in the morning before I would fall into a dream-disturbed sleep. Renal failure can also effect the body temperature so I often felt cold. Driving in a car or being in an enclosed space often made me feel sick. The dreaded diet returned with its restrictions of fluid, salt, protein and potassium. The impurities in my system made concentration difficult but I tried to read the Bible each day. One time I read Jeremiah's Lament:

> I am a man who has seen affliction . . . *He* has driven me away and made me walk in darkness rather than light.

I wrote to my friends:

> What struck me about this is that Jeremiah is talking about his own real 'Christian' experience. It's quite shocking to read that 'He' made me walk in darkness.
>
> It's easy for Christians to communicate that everything is always rosy in their lives. 'Rejoice in the Lord,' Paul tells us, but I don't think this means absence of sorrow. Paul also said that he was 'sorrowful yet always rejoicing'. I have done some study on the word 'joy' in the Bible and concluded that it is fundamentally a positive attitude — sometimes this can lead to feeling happy or good and even laughter. In adverse circumstances we can retain this positive attitude but we will also feel sorrow. In other words joy and sorrow are not mutually exclusive feelings.
>
> Sometimes Christians give me the impression that worship is a light-hearted experience with joy being the

only legitimate emotion. In his deepest sorrow because of the loss of all that was dear to him Job said, 'The Lord has given, the Lord has taken away. Blessed be the name of the Lord.' Jeremiah experienced 'walking in darkness rather than light', but he also continued to trust God and to acknowledge his goodness.

I think that this is how we felt. We have felt hurt, angry, bewildered, ill, sometimes depressed but in the midst of this we've known that God is good and will work out his perfect plan for us. Sometimes we don't see God very clearly but we really have seen his love in you and want to thank you for your expressions of love.

After three months of dialysing in the hospital I was pleased to be able to now have the treatment at home. Once again, as in Sheffield, the National Health Service prepared a room in our house costing around £3,000. Waterproof flooring, shelving for all the equipment, an alarm system, separate electricity, phone and water supply were installed in one of the first-floor bedrooms. It is easy to complain about the NHS but providing this life-support system cost £2,500 a year to run.

For me it was a great relief to be able to dialyse at home but for Sandra it meant pressure she would have preferred not to have. Though she had some training at the hospital on the procedures it was more the sense of responsibility she dreaded. She lived in fear of the alarm. If I needed anything whilst dialysing the only way I could get her attention was by pulling the alarm cord above my bed. In the early days, she would run

Renal Failure Again (1989)

upstairs, come into the room to switch it off, not knowing if it was a serious emergency or if I just wanted a drink. We eventually discovered that 'baby monitors' could be a very useful communication tool saving Sandra unnecessary panic. At other times the alarm would need to be rung for more serious matters like a sudden loss of blood pressure accompanied by severe leg cramps and breathing difficulties. Then Sandra would need to administer saline into my blood stream as quickly as possible.

The pressure on her was tremendous and I was so helpless to know what to do. It hurt me deeply to cause her so much pain. I knew that she suffered much stress because of the pressure. I knew the fears had returned about how long I would live. I knew that by nature, she is a person who acutely feels other people's pain and of course mine especially.

One thing we really dreaded was the rare occasions when impurities would get into the bloodstream. When this happened I would begin to feel cold and shivery and would end up shaking quite violently. I had learned from previous experience that it would necessitate coming off the machine earlier. I would not want to stop dialysis too quickly because that would mean that I would have to dialyse again the next day to make up for the inadequate treatment. I could see Sandra's distress as the symptoms grew worse and would try to reassure her that it would be all right the next day. The words didn't seem to help and her increasing anxiety would make me cry, then we would both end up crying because of each other's pain. This didn't help my vision or the concentration needed for the disconnecting procedure!

She did have an excellent women's support group from Emmanuel-St. James Church with whom she could talk, laugh or cry. One time they were having a discussion about the difficulty of making the right choices. 'I don't feel as if I have any *choices*,' Sandra blurted out and began to cry. Her life was being dominated by my dialysis and Mark's diabetes not to mention the normal running of a busy home.

An improvement in the support structure from the hospital was the allocation of a home nurse, Linda, who would visit us at home to discuss how things were going with the both of us. She was very kind and concerned but formidable. If anything needed arranging with the hospital she would make sure things were done! This meant a real improvement because at the out-patients clinic no questions would be asked about how Sandra was coping.

The regular out-patient visit would usually involve getting weighed, having blood pressure taken, giving some blood for tests, waiting for an hour or two to see the doctor (often a different one from the time before) to tell him how I was and what medication I was on. (This I never understood as they were the ones who prescribed the medicine and had the records in front of them.) I was usually then given an explanation of the cause of the particular difficulty I was presently facing but often nothing could be done.

I was then given a prescription to take to the pharmacy which meant another hour's wait. Later due to cut-backs we had to order our prescriptions from our own GP. The medicine was actually more expensive to the NHS this way because a doctor in a local practice couldn't get cost reductions for buying in bulk. The hospitals had to cut back on expenses so did this by moving as many prescriptions as possible to the GP's budget. That's National Health economics for you!

We tried to keep our lives as happy as possible for ourselves and for our now young adults. Sandra and I would eat out about once a week and go out for a special evening from time to time helped by the Attendance Allowance we received. Some years earlier I had been introduced to opera through seeing Zeffirelli's *La Traviata* starring Placido Domingo and was totally hooked.

I have Zeffirelli to thank for introducing me to Shakespeare through his great film, *Romeo and Juliet*, not to mention a new appreciation of Christ through *Jesus of Nazareth*.

We especially looked forward to the visit of the Glyndebourne Company because they displayed a translation of the text on a small screen above the stage. They realised that there were other people like us who didn't understand Italian or French and wanted to follow the storyline.

Manchester has so many cultural activities. We saw Torvill and Dean at the newly opened G-Mex, the converted Central Railway Station. The Manchester theatres put on grand shows like *Phantom of the Opera* and *Les Misérables* both of which were very moving, with more than a few tears shed. The *Messiah* at the Free Trade Hall performed by the Hallé Orchestra and Chorus was an event we attended whenever we could. This is my favourite piece of music and I never tire of listening to it. If I'm not weeping over the strains of 'Come unto me, all ye that labour and are heavy laden', it will be 'Behold and see, if there be any sorrow like unto my sorrow'. At the other end of the cultural spectrum was the Christmas Pantomime, starring Les Dawson.

Mandy and I attended a concert of the Hothouse Flowers at the Apollo and although we both liked their music we had very different reactions. She was dancing and having a great time while some of their sad songs made me cry. 'The older you are, the harder it gets,' sang their barefooted, Irish lead singer, Liam O'Moanlai. I could relate to that but Mandy said, 'You're a big softie, Dad!' We were both particularly struck by their version of a Crosby, Stills and Nash song called, *I can see clearly now*, little realising its future significance to us.

It was especially good for Sandra when we were able to get away for a proper holiday where someone else could look after the dialysis. When I first had renal failure in the seventies there were very few opportunities available but now I was able to dialyse in hospitals as far away as Majorca and Tenerife. I still had to keep to the dietary restrictions but at least Sandra was totally free from the pressure for a while.

One of the greatest escapes to me was working in the garden. I had strategically placed chairs situated around the garden so that I could sit down if I ran out of energy. Digging was difficult with a haemoglobin of five or six. I would turn over a few spadefuls and then sit down, rest a while, get up, and do a few more spadefuls. A recently acquired smaller border spade was very helpful. I especially enjoyed the creative aspects of gardening like arranging plants in complementary colours and shapes. Sandra was a great help here with her feel for colour and form.

Thinking creatively about the different seasons opened up some new dimensions to gardening for me. The white winter sun made the coloured bark of the young Dogwood radiate in red and gold flame. Flowering spring bulbs heralded balmier days. My dad would bring over bulbs from Holland, usually exceeding his weight allowance and probably heavier than he was supposed to carry at his age too. Summer boasted with its abundance of colour in the borders but autumn wouldn't let itself be overshadowed, going out in a blaze of glory.

I had a greenhouse so that tomatoes could be grown in the summer and tender plants over-wintered. No shop-bought tomato compares with a home-grown cherry tomato like Sungold or the beefsteak Big Boy. I grew cordons of apple trees, fan-trained pears and delicious plums on dwarf rootstock like Victoria, greengages and damsons. Fortunately, Sandra could make wonderful jam out of these fruits. Freshly picked strawberries with cream are truly one of the high points of the season. I had beds with a variety of vegetables like sprouts, onions and beans too. It never ceased to amaze me that all these things grew out of small, dry seeds. Truly a miracle of God's creation.

We had some spare land at the far end of the garden where we kept a few chickens – that was if the urban fox didn't get them. All the family loved the fresh eggs soft-boiled. Great for dipping 'soldiers' of toast into.

Nothing was ever wasted in the van Zuylen household. Food scraps went to the chickens, other biodegradable waste went on the compost heap and any spare wood was burnt in the log fire in the hall. Stephen's nickname for me was 'Recycle Man'.

Friday evenings were set aside for Geoff Hamilton and *Gardener's World* and any other gardening programme that was on. I learnt nearly everything I know about gardening from these programmes.

Mandy, Mark and Stephen were a great help to us. I was particularly interested to notice how each of them showed their care for me in my illness in a different way. If I was on the machine when Stephen came home from school he would pop his head round the door, ask me how I was and exchange a few words. It was hard for him to see me on dialysis but this did not stop him from coming into the room for a little chat.

Mark didn't ask very much but related to me in a 'pally' way. His approach seemed to have the sense of 'You and me, we know what it's like to suffer'.

Mandy was lively and cheerful and would try to create a pleasant atmosphere around the house when she was home from Newcastle. She rarely, if ever, came into the kidney room – it was just too painful for her sensitive, caring compassionate nature.

The internal bleeding had continued from time to time since the beginning of the year and my haemoglobin started to drop causing me to feel gradually weaker. It took eight months for the hospital to call me in for the haemorrhoids operation regardless of Dr Joe's urging them to do a colonoscopy. These were seen to and yet I continued to loose blood. Clearly the haemorrhoids were not the only cause of bleeding.

Again my doctor urged a colonoscopy to have a proper look inside. When this was eventually done a polyp was discovered but I was assured that it could be easily removed. I was soon called in again to have the offending polyp removed but it didn't prove to be as simple as expected. 'I was not able to remove it because it is a little larger than I expected,' the doctor performing the operation informed me. 'We have sent some cells off for analysis but think it's benign so there is probably nothing to worry about. A minor operation will be needed to remove it.' Benign polyp? I wasn't even sure what this was exactly but was afraid to ask.

A few days later the report came back that the polyp was in fact malignant, regardless of previous reassurances. I just couldn't believe it! Two potentially life-threatening illnesses at the same time.

The operation was done to remove a small section of my colon. The discovery of cancer also meant that I was removed from the transplant list.

After the operation I felt very weak and had no desire to eat. Even though I didn't really eat anything I was told I still needed to dialyse. 'Why do I need to dialyse if I'm not eating anything?' I asked angrily. 'Dr Popoudopalis made the arrangements you'll have to ask him,' the nurse said. It was explained to me that even when not eating the body still produces substances that need dialysing out.

So over to renal unit I went, waiting in a draughty corridor for what seemed like ages until a bed was ready for the treatment. I lay in that hospital bed deeply frustrated, dialysing, tubes running in and out, powerless to do anything about my situation. Thankfully the nurses put the needles in for me, something they usually expected an experienced patient to do for himself.

I found the hospital food very unappetising and couldn't be bothered to eat. No salt, no taste, colourless, cooked to death, incredible combinations of food, looking and smelling awful. (If you've been in the situation, you know what I mean.) I do not understand why patients who are so desperately in need of nourishment are served up with such inedible food.

'You know what I feel like,' I said to Sandra, 'some of that nice beef tea you've made for me before when I've been ill.' Pleased that there was something I fancied she bought some good beef from the local butcher and put it on to boil. After some time she drained off the nourishing and delicious stock ready to be poured into a flask. When she returned to the kitchen later to do this she arrived just in time to see the neighbour's cat,

Renal Failure Again (1989)

Amy, licking her lips and scurrying out the door! She had lapped it all up! 'What am I going to do? Perhaps Dirk will like the bits of beef that are left?' Sandra brought the remnants of my 'healing potion' into the hospital. I didn't want Sandra to feel even worse about the situation so I said, 'It smells nice enough, perhaps I'll just try some.' It did taste nice but it was not nice to my stomach. It landed like lead and I felt like vomiting. After Sandra left I rushed to the toilet and was violently sick. Holding onto my stomach with its fifteen stitches, my stomach retching, is an experience I won't forget very quickly. I consoled myself with murderous thoughts about Amy!

Mandy's memories of visiting me in hospital are very vivid. She recalled to me later the shock seeing me looking so yellow and gaunt. 'Like a skeleton,' she said, 'You looked so horrific to me, a shadow of your former self. All the time I wanted to cry but was embarrassed because we were in a hospital. A tear would run down my cheek as I walked out but I felt I couldn't release the emotion inside. By the time I had driven home the ability to cry had been lost and it took me many years to release the feeling.'

I returned home 10 kilos lighter. My leg muscles were so weak that I could amuse myself by tapping them and watching them flop from side to side.

I was very touched by the concern and interest of our neighbours. One of them, Ron Stout, a consultant at Christie's Cancer Hospital was particularly reassuring and helpful.

Now, where's that cat?

15

Darkness (1990–92)

'Stay with me'
Shakespeare's Sister

Articles had begun to appear in the medical press about a new wonder drug that could raise the haemoglobin levels of kidney patients. In America, it was making an enormous difference to the quality of life of those who took it. We were very excited to hear about this development but unfortunately it was not available to patients here. Some of my Navigator colleagues had heard about my need for this drug and were looking into making arrangements to have the drug sent over, with them footing the bill. Treatment cost about £25.00 a week. We were deeply touched by their kindness and generosity.

However, as we were looked into this possibility we heard that trials were also beginning in Britain. The NHS would not set aside money for the trials so it was sponsored by the drug company which produced Erythropoietin. 'Epo' as we called it, is a hormone that the kidneys produce to stimulate the production of red cells. Of course, when renal failure takes place this substance is no longer produced thereby significantly reducing the number of cells that carry oxygen around the body, hence the lack of energy.

This treatment made an immediate and sustained difference to my energy levels but what would happen when the trials finished? I couldn't even begin to think about it. The government would still make no new money available for the drug even though they knew of its life-changing effect. If GPs wanted to re-direct some of their limited resources to the provision of this drug, well that was up to them. Some did prescribe it and some didn't, but thankfully mine did. Was I grateful? You better believe it!

My haemoglobin had been raised but new problems began to appear. Most mornings I would be woken up very early with severe pains in my hand and wrist. It was so painful I had to get out of bed, rubbing my hands and wrist and pacing the floor, not that it made any difference. It always took an hour or two for the pain to go away.

At every hospital visit I would bring up the problem but nobody seemed worried. Finally it was decided to send me to a neurologist who ran a series of tests looking at my nerve functions. 'The high levels of impurities in your blood over so many years have caused some irreversible nerve damage. I'm afraid that there isn't much we can do,' he said.

I did have occasional injections of steroids into my wrist but this gave only temporary relief. The rheumatologist told me that this couldn't be done too frequently because of possible side effects.

Eventually carpal tunnel syndrome was diagnosed. Nerves from the arm pass through a 'tunnel' of ligament to the hand and fingers. In my case the nerves were being constricted because of a build-up of impurities and so ligaments needed to be cut to relieve the pressure.

This was eventually done by the consultant Mr Johnson under a local anaesthetic. I know I wasn't supposed to feel anything but I had the distinct sense that I could feel everything he was doing.

The effect of renal failure was visible to them. 'Notice how dry it is,' he said to his students, 'normally it should be red with healthy cells'.

After the operation Mr Johnson assured me that things would be better and for a while they were. The only problem was that a year later the same problem developed in my other wrist. This time however, I was quickly seen to and thankfully the operation was done under a general anaesthetic. It always took me a long time to get over a general anaesthetic, in fact months. It wasn't that I really felt poorly all that time but when I looked back I would realise that I wasn't one hundred per cent. Having said that, did I ever feel a hundred per cent?!

I won't forget the first week of June in 1990 too quickly! On Friday whilst I was dialysing, impurities got into the system causing an infection. Usually I needed a day or two to recover but because Saturday was the wedding day of the son and daughter of two couples who were friends of ours, we felt we should go. This meant that Sandra had to drive all the way from Manchester to Newmarket.

When we returned the next day it wasn't long before I was on my way to Leeds to see Mandy, who had been in a motorcycle accident. She had a broken arm and some bad bruising but thankfully God spared her life. The motorbike, on which she was a passenger was travelling at 50 miles an hour and ran straight into the side of a car that had wrongly pulled out in front of them. She was thrown over the bonnet and onto the road, but thankfully there were no oncoming cars at the time.

On Monday Stephen burst into our bedroom with tears streaming down his cheeks informing us that someone had broken into our garage and stolen his precious mountain bike. It was his pride and joy because he had built the valuable bike himself.

The next day Mark had a minor car accident but was unhurt. Both Mark and Stephen had a bad dose of flu that week too.

Sandra and I had made a start at getting back involved with Navigator activities. I had virtually been out of work for two years now and found that I had limited emotional energy. Sandra too felt that she had very little to give. We felt like the little boy who brought his few loaves and fishes to Jesus. It wasn't enough, but he took it, blessed it, and miraculously fed five thousand people. We gave to Jesus what we had and trusted him to multiply it to the benefit of others.

We had a very relaxing holiday in Sussex that summer. We stayed in a bungalow that was somewhat sub-standard to say the least but after getting used to it we laughed it off and slummed it for two weeks. We had mostly sunny weather and were grateful that Stephen found friends to hang around with.

This was my first experience of a British holiday camp. We had chosen to go to the Sussex Beach Holiday Village because there were dialysis facilities provided by the BKPA in the grounds. The British Kidney Patients Association do a tremendous amount of good work helping patients and their families. The 'luxury' cabin was the first shock. Upon opening the door we were overwhelmed by the stale smell that assaulted our nostrils. The carpet fitter had had the novel idea of not only laying carpet on the floor but also half way up the wall, thus making any further decoration unnecessary! No use wasting good money on wallpaper or a picture! The orange plastic upright chairs around the table served the dual purpose of being lounge chairs as well.

The facility was self-catering but food could also be purchased at the Wild West Bar. Nightly entertainment was provided and we were cordially invited to come and enjoy ourselves. I wasn't that keen but decided that perhaps I needed to go to broaden my experience of English culture.

Now it has to be said the English at the seaside are something of a mystery to me. What is the pleasure

Darkness (1990–92)

of sitting on a pebbled beach in the drizzly rain? Why do they laugh at such second-rate comedians? What is so funny about wearing silly hats? What is the appeal of shows that feature singers and dancers that failed their auditions for the West End shows? 'The Sussex Beach Holiday Village is proud to present the show-stoppers from *Starlight Express*.' I hate to admit it, but we quite enjoyed that show!

The 'highlight' of our time was the kidney patients' coach trip to the Isle of Wight. Every patient had a 'renal' horror story to tell. One had more hospital visits than anyone, another the most unpleasant side effects, and another had nearly died too many times to count. Some had trouble walking, others had trouble eating, another breathing difficulties. It reminded me of the famed *Yorkshiremen* sketch;

> Who would have thought thirty years ago we would be here at Sussex Holiday Beach with a fluid restriction, eh?
>
> Aye – in them days we were lucky to have any fluid at all.
>
> Aye – a cup of cold tea.
>
> Without milk, because that contained protein, but we were allowed sugar.
>
> You were lucky to have a cup to drink out of. We had to drink out of a rolled-up newspaper.
>
> The best we could manage was to suck on a piece of damp cloth.
>
> But you know we were happy in those days – even though we had a restricted diet . . .

We turned down the opportunity to go on another day outing! The positive side effect of the trip was that I felt comparatively very young and healthy.

But to be honest things were still hard. At Christmas Sandra wrote:

I was struck by the words in Habakkak 3 verse 19 –

> The Sovereign Lord is my strength;
> He makes my feet like the feet of a deer,
> He enables me to go to the heights.

As we look back over the year it seems that we have been surrounded by insurmountable mountains. Difficulties in every direction. We have felt deplete of human strength, tired, angry, upset, overwhelmed, wishing our circumstances were different. The mountains are still there, our strength is weak but we know that God is giving us the strength to climb those mountains.

We have many things to be thankful for:

1. Dirk's energy is greater now that he has the Erythropoietin.
2. All the tests for cancer have been negative, the prognosis is good.
3. Dirk has been put back on the transplant list.
4. Dirk is able to resume work to a limited degree.
5. Mandy's arm is regaining strength since the accident.
6. God has continued to meet our financial needs, using many of you to do this.

We are very thankful. God does not promise any of us an easy life; as Christians we are not exempt from difficult circumstances. Let us all learn together to climb the mountains of life, which can be so daunting, with his strength and not let them overwhelm us.

What Sandra didn't know at that time was about a conversation that eighteen-year-old Mark and I had together.

'Could I have a word with you, Dad?'

'Yeah, sure let's go into the front room.'

Mark paced the floor like an animal in a cage and then suddenly blurted out, 'My girlfriend is pregnant!'

'Er, what girl friend? I didn't know you had one.' Bringing girls home to meet his Mum and Dad was not part of his usual routine. Mark told me that his girlfriend's name was Halima, she was older than him and already had an eight-year-old daughter. She was now three months pregnant.

I couldn't quite believe it or take it in but assured him that we would give him all the support we could. He came over and gave me a big hug. As we held each other I told him I would tell Sandra, when the time seemed right. He didn't want me to tell her right away or mention it to any other member of the family either. It was a real burden to carry alone and especially during Christmas celebrations.

Visiting Mandy gave Sandra and me an opportunity to have extended time together. We had travelled up to Newcastle but I couldn't get my head together or find a way to tell her. Arranging to meet Mandy near the University we spotted her a long way off! Her big, floor-length coat blowing open in the wind striding towards us in her Doc Marten boots a big smile on her face. The only difference from the last time we saw her was that her hair was now purple. She greeted us in her usual warm, extravagant way, hugs all around. We had a good time together but all the time Mark's situation was on my mind.

Sandra and I went to Bainbridges for a cup of coffee. I had to tell her. No circumstance seemed to be appropriate so I just blurted it all out. Like me, she didn't know how to take it in either. It all seemed a bit unreal especially not even having met the mother-to-be. One thing for sure, the pleasure had gone out of the Christmas preparations.

Mark told Mandy and Stephen his news but we felt we ought to tell my parents and were particularly worried as to what they would think. We wondered how they would respond to Mark, of whom they were very fond, needing to set up home with someone at his age and under these circumstances. We needn't have worried, their response greatly helped us. 'You know,' my Dad said, 'this may be an opportunity for you to show her Christ's love.' What a challenge! How did Christ show his love to people? He was a friend and helper.

In my lighter moments I had to smile as I thought of one of my initial attempts at 'sex education' with Mark, especially warning him about older women. He was eleven or twelve years old and I noticed that he was hanging around with older girls whose figures

Darkness (1990–92)

were beginning to develop and some of them were wearing quite provocative clothing. 'You need to talk to him,' Sandra instructed me, 'it's your responsibility!' I was looking for an opportunity to bring it up casually. I didn't want to be heavy-handed about it!

We used to shower together in those days (I am a modest man and would wear my bathing costume), and so I took the opportunity to have a word with him. 'You need to be careful about getting involved with older women,' I said hoping to leave it at that. 'Why is that, Dad?' 'Well . . . er . . . they can be a bit . . . you know . . . sexy.' (Pause) 'You mean like Mum?' What did he mean? Did he mean older, because Sandra was a little older than me or did he mean sexy, like his Mum? I didn't have the nerve to ask so we left it at that.

We were seeking to cope with the usual stresses of life with dialysis, and Mark's situation added substantially to the pressure we felt. We felt we were just daily trying to keep our heads above water, clinging to our life raft, God.

During this time, however, God did lift me up in an unusual way. I had a consultation with Dr Gokal, who asked various questions about the symptoms I was experiencing. As I was telling him these things I realised that I had in fact given up. I wasn't trying to overcome the difficulties anymore. The effect was like hitting my head on the floor and the shock of it bouncing me up again. When you hit bottom you can only go upwards. I realised that I needed to appropriate more of God's strength and pull myself together. I especially felt I needed to do more to support Sandra because I was dragging her down with me.

My change of attitude didn't make everything appear rosy, but I noticed that I didn't dread having visitors as much. I enjoyed and benefited from people when they actually came. The problem was more one of the fearful anticipation of seeing people rather than their actual visit.

At other times people would phone and ask how I was. 'Oh, all right thanks,' and I'd hope to leave it at that. Sometimes I would think, 'Well, to really tell you how I feel would take too long and you probably don't want to know. If you really do want to know, I don't know if I want to tell you.' It made me feel even worse talking about it because it focused my mind on the difficulties. Some of my friends did confide that they sometimes found my lack of communication trying.

I read in the local kidney patients' magazine:

> The start of a recent telephone conversation between two kidney patients tickled my sense of humour. If you think along similar lines it might raise a smile.
>
> Hello – It's me.
> Oh hello – how are you?
> I'm alright
>
> That's one of the best words in the English language. It can mean anything from I am almost completely shattered, on one hand, to I am reasonably well on the other.

Well, I am some way off from being completely shattered although I am far from being reasonably well.
Oh, I see, you are alright then?
Yes I am alright.
Good.

I cried when I read that article not because there was no little humour in it but because it related too much to my experience.

On a visit to the hospital I had asked Dr Joe, 'Am I a sick man who is trying to do a bit of work or a well person who isn't quite up to scratch.' He answered that he was allowing me to do some work in order to keep me sane. What he meant was that even though I was officially 'off sick', for my own sake I needed to be involved with others. I had certainly found this to be true. It was an encouragement to see how God used my time with people and blessed me in the activities I participated in no matter how minimal. Sandra too had the same experience. I often thought of the boy with the totally inadequate food supply which he brought to Jesus, and saw him multiply it to feed a multitude.

Another thing I was needing to learn about was accepting our children as they were. I observed that acceptance was often based on academic or sporting or other achievements. I prided myself in accepting my children on the basis of who they were rather than their achievements but then discovered a flaw in my thinking. I asked myself, 'Would I accept my children even if they violated my deeply held Christian convictions?' I realised that living a Christian life meant more to me than academic, sporting, or other achievements.

I asked Mandy if she felt any pressure from me to behave in a certain way. Somehow I hoped the answer would be, 'No, I feel completely free and accepted by you.' The unexpected answer was 'Yes, I do feel pressure from you.' I realised I needed to affirm, love and accept whether I approved of their decisions or not. This is the way God treats us.

Though the situation with Mark and Halima started so traumatically things became very different as time passed by. In fact one of the greatest joys at the time was being involved with Mark and his newly acquired family. Kyle, who was born in May, was such a bundle of joy. He was a very happy and contented baby. After the initial shock of becoming 'grandparents' Sandra and I were really enjoying it. We were also introduced to Halima's daughter, Natalie, aged nine who was a real live wire. She called me 'Granddad Dirk'.

The birth of our grandson was not exactly at the time or under the circumstances we expected but we were beginning to see God's goodness to us in this situation. When I told my mother about the birth of Kyle she said, 'Perhaps God has given you this child to bring some joy into your lives.'

Mark moved in with Halima and showed tremendous dedication to them even being a father to Natalie, who saw very little of her natural father. To be honest I have never seen a man give himself to his

Darkness (1990–92)

family like Mark did in those days. He was only nineteen and effectively married with a family of two children.

The new family was very special to Sandra and me. I related very much to the Bible story of Jacob and his son Benjamin. Kyle was to me similar to what Benjamin was to his father. When he was born under tragic circumstances his mother gave him a name which means 'son of my trouble', but his father Jacob changed it to Benjamin, which means 'son of my right hand'. What started as 'trouble' became a source of strength. It was said of Jacob that 'his life was bound up in the lad's life'. My life was bound up with Kyle's too.

God gave us a child in our darkest days to bring us joy in our pain. Stephen in 1976 and Kyle in 1991.

My energy often didn't extend further than the wider family. I found it increasingly difficult to socialise. The worst scenario was if there was a party coming up. For days there would be a sense of dread and foreboding and I would only go to please Sandra.

I have noticed that when a bird or animal has been seriously hurt it retires to a quite place to recover. There is a need for stillness and solitude. I think this is how I felt. I just needed to be alone to recover. I wanted to be alone and escape into the world of books, television and music.

For me music taps into my own deepest feelings. I can cry at music without words or even words that I don't understand. The female voice especially can touch me deeply and none more so at the time than

'Shakespeare's Sister' with the song 'Stay with me.' When Sandra and I saw the video on television we could hardly bear to watch it. The video heightened the power of the music.

A woman dressed in white is hovering protectively over an obviously sick man lying on a stretcher singing:

> If this world is wearing thin and you're thinking of escape,
> I'll go anywhere with you, just wrap me up in chains
> But if you try to go alone don't think I'll understand.
> Stay with me, stay with me.
> In the silence of your room, in the darkness of your dream
> You must only think of me, there can be none in between . . .
> Stay with me . . .

At this point a darkly dressed witch-like woman came into view singing in a lower voice:

> You'd better hope and pray that you'll make it safe back to your own world . . .
> 'Coz when you sleep at night they don't hear your cries in your own world
> Only time will tell if you can break the spell back in your own world.

Once again the woman in white would sing plaintively, over and over again as she held onto her man: 'Stay, stay, stay, stay . . .'

We worked very hard at not letting our lives be dominated by illness but it wasn't easy. From time to time Sandra would think about getting a job outside the home. At just the right time she heard about a course at Manchester Cathedral designed to help people know themselves better, to consider what motivates them and what influences their choices. It is called the Myers-Briggs Type Indicator Course and was led by Canon Bruce Duncan.

One of the tests that was done was to consider a rose. Each person had to write down what they saw. One saw a simple flower, another a symbol of love and another focused more on the colour or texture. This highlighted the different ways we view what we see. The tests showed that Sandra was strong in sensing and feeling. She likes to touch, smell, taste and see. It became clear that Sandra is a person who is energised and stimulated through her contact with people. She is very sensitive to people, sympathetic, adaptable and responsive. I am more the kind of person who likes to be on my own, setting and achieving my own goals, overcoming obstacles. I am sensitive but like to work things through in my mind. My more introverted ways accentuated by illness had closed doors for Sandra who was always adapting to me. Obviously she did this out of the kindness of her heart but we realised it had gone too far. Because Sandra is so adaptable, she adapted too much to my character which in effect and unintentionally stopped her from being herself. The carer can become the victim and end up being unable to 'care' any more.

Sandra considered looking for a job as a medical technician but felt that she had enough contact with hospitals!

She had always been interested in colour, whether it be the clothes she wears or the rooms she decorates. She had read some books about colour as it related to clothing and make-up. This had been very useful in her own choosing of cosmetics and clothing. She is also a very capable seamstress so this was very useful as well. Sandra enjoyed making clothes for herself and others.

She responded to an advert in a local newspaper about setting up as a colour and image consultant with 'Beauty for all Seasons'. She received training and how to help clients choose the make-up that suits them best.

This work is tailor-made for Sandra and has brought some necessary relief and pleasure into her life, to say nothing about the enhanced appearance of her clients. She is also able to advise them on the style of clothing that suits their body shape and the colours that make them look their best. New terms like 'illusion dressing' entered her vocabulary which I understand has to do with disguising the less desirable aspects of a particular woman's figure. Best not go into too much detail here! These matters are outside my ability to comprehend!

From my point of view however things were getting worse and worse. My energy levels were going down again. I felt depressed most of the time.

On a visit to a doctor about a pilonidal sinus I had, he said to me, 'You seem depressed, do you want to come back another time to talk about it?' I turned down his offer thinking, 'What good will talking do! The reason I'm depressed is because of this *damned* dialysis and there is nothing you can do about that.'

Reading my Bible brought no real comfort except perhaps when I read how Job felt:

> If I go to the east, he is not there;
> If I go to the west I do not find him.
> When he is at work in the north, I do not see him;
> When he turns to the south I catch no glimpse of him.

At least I wasn't the only one who felt like that! Every morning I spent some time reading the Bible but nothing seemed to help me, as it had so often done in the past. David had written in one of his Psalms, 'If you remain silent, I shall be like those who have gone down to the pit.' That was how I felt, like someone in a pit to whom God is silent.

Part of the problem was the impurity levels in my system and the way they affected my ability to concentrate or remember. For example, frequently I would go into one of the rooms in the house and not know why I was there. Little 'humorous' comments like, 'Oh, I have the same problem too, we're all getting a bit older you know, ha, ha, ha.' This comment would particularly irritate me because it made me feel even more isolated and misunderstood.

Another difficulty was that though I still could have intelligent (though I have no proof of that!) conversations with my colleagues I wasn't really properly involved. I would comment on situations not really understanding the implications of what I was saying. This led to some difficulties later when people would remind me that I had said things of which I had no recollection whatsoever.

Sexually, things were not going very well either. Dr Joe offered to make an appointment for me to see a sex therapist but a combination of pride and hopelessness held me back. 'What can she tell me that I don't already know? I advise people on their sex lives myself!' Eventually, in despair I asked if an appointment could be made for Sandra and me to see her. We made a few visits which were a real help to us.

In the seventies and again this time I worked very hard not to let dialysis dominate our lives but it wasn't working anymore. I felt I was getting a beating three times a week and couldn't handle it any more. I prayed to God again and again, 'Save me from this s**t life!'

There were so many side effects to cope with. The itching, the insomnia, the restlessness, the nausea, the headaches and sore shoulders. I was taking tablets to cope with the side effects of other tablets, about 25 a day. Some kidney patients, like myself, had a mild form of osteoporosis – a lack of absorption of calcium – which necessitated taking 18 tablets a day just for that!

I was vulnerable to infections which sometimes necessitated hospitalisation. One time when I was in hospital with a very high temperature and a bit delirious a young nurse was trying to find out from me what tablets I was on and the dosage. I could only think of one or two and had no idea of the quantity. 'Is he always like this?' the nurse asked Sandra. She explained that I usually did know exactly what tablets I was on and the dose but that I wasn't feeling too well at the time! It seemed so absurd to be asked for this kind of information along with a detailed medical history when there was so much documentation available already in my bulging hospital notes.

My tolerance of pain seemed to be decreasing and I found the needling an increasing hurdle. It didn't even hurt that much because by this time the scar tissue had desensitised the area used for putting in the needles. It was more the idea itself and the fear of accidents.

Dr Joe admitted to me later that it disturbed him when he saw me at the clinic because he knew there was actually little that could be done for me. What I needed was a transplant and there was lengthening waiting list for these. (The waiting list is not so much a queue as a register. Decisions were made on the basis of suitability determined by blood and tissue type.)

Dr Joe was always especially good with me, always taking the time to answer questions and explain what was going on with my body. Sometimes doctors can treat patients as if they are socially and intellectually deficient. This may in fact be true, but I found it encouraging when a doctor credited me with having a few 'little grey cells' too! The approach of 'Trust me, I'm a doctor!' doesn't work too well in a hospital environment where their mistakes are known and discussed by patients. I feel very fortunate in having had such good treatment by the renal staff and my GP Bill Tamkin especially.

I found the staff who do the initial preparatory work, like taking blood samples and blood pressure in the out-patients clinic, thoughtful and interested in my welfare. One of the receptionists, Marion, was particularly a 'sight for sore eyes'. Her good looks and cheerful manner made even the most inhuman wreck feel that life might be worthwhile after all.

For me, I felt for the first time in my life that I saw death on the horizon and I can't say that it was an unattractive option. If it wasn't for my family needing, wanting and loving me I'm sure I would have given up and allowed the renal failure to take its course. It wouldn't have been difficult . . .

I of course wasn't the only one in pain. For Mandy this was an especially dark time. She later told Sandra and me that she felt completely unable to cope. She started having panic attacks though she didn't know what they were at the time and so found them even more frightening. She felt no one could understand or help her and so felt very alone in her suffering. To add to the pressure, Mandy felt she was being a terrible burden to us. She just wanted to escape back to Newcastle to lose herself in student life. It didn't work of course but this was the only way she felt she could cope. It took some years before she could face and work through her feelings with the help of a counsellor.

Darkness (1990–92)

Close friends and even some of the doctors later confided in me that they didn't think I had long to live. My friend, Ron Finlay, came home from a visit and said to Bette his wife, with tears in his eyes, 'Dirk's not long for this world'. Thankfully God was working something out for me that I had no thought or expectation about.

16

The Second Transplant (1992)

> 'I can see clearly now'
> *Hothouse Flowers*

'Your sister Wilma wants to donate one of her kidneys to you. She has thought very carefully about this and you need to respect her decision. In fact, she is very sure that God wants her to do this!'

You may be surprised that Sandra presented Wilma's idea to me so forcibly, but she knew her husband! Even though the idea of a transplant from my other sister, Mary had been considered in the 70s I really wasn't willing to have anyone in the family put themselves at risk for my sake. I felt vindicated in this because Mary later had some health problems herself. Since that time the possibility of a transplant from a family member had never crossed my mind.

I didn't know how to react to the offer but said to Sandra that the possibility could be looked into. I said to myself, with my customary humility, 'Well, if God has spoken to her so clearly he will have to speak to me as well!'

My main concern was the risk that Wilma would be taking. It would involve a major operation for her with considerable time needed to recover. And what about if it was all in vain? Why couldn't God just provide me with a suitable kidney from someone who had died? Then no one would need to take any risks.

The next day I carried on in my Bible reading from where I had left off the day before. I was now up to Esther, the third book in a trilogy about the Babylonian captivity of the Jews. Esther, a Jewess, had been chosen to be Queen by the ruler, Xerxes. Not long after this the king had approved a major plot to destroy all the Jews living in the kingdom. He was unaware of Esther's nationality at the time. Esther's uncle, Mordecai, appealed to her to speak to the king on behalf of her people. This was not as easy as it sounds because if she arrived in court uninvited she could be put to death unless the King gave special permission to enter. Mordecai's reply stood out to me:

> If you keep quiet at a time like this, help will come from somewhere for the Jews, and they will be saved, but you will die and your father's family will come to an end. Yet who knows – maybe it was for a time like this that you were made Queen!

God could deliver me some other way i.e. a cadaver transplant but perhaps Wilma's offer was meant for 'a time like this'. Had he put her in this position of being able to save me? This was an offer to save my life! I was in no position to refuse.

I felt free now to proceed with this possibility but guarded my emotions very carefully so as not to get my hopes up too much. I felt that the past had taught me to expect the worst.

Wilma, who lives in Holland, came over to do tests that spring and amazingly everything was as good as it could possibly be. Wilma's health was excellent and the kidney was a near-perfect match, only an identical twin could have been better. The surgeon Mr Parrott, set September 11 as the likely date for the transplant.

I knew that she felt strongly that this was something she ought to do so I asked her how she had come to her decision.

She told me that the first time she had thought about it was fifteen years earlier, just after her first daughter, Naomi, had been born. It was a time when she was desperately trying to find out what God wanted her to do with her life. She always had the feeling that she wasn't doing enough to help others. She felt obligated to do everything that came her way and even considered adopting a child in need. She had a continual sense of frustration and confusion about what to do with her life.

What really helped her was a sermon at church about Ananias, who helped Paul after he became blind on the Damascus Road. God clearly spoke to Ananias directing him to help Paul and that is what he did! She suddenly realised that she didn't need to seek in desperation and hopelessness but could live in a more relaxed way focusing on those things that she did know God wanted her to do. She could trust God to make clear what she needed to do when the time came. Even though she wanted to help me she had no sense that she should do so at this time. A huge burden was lifted off her shoulders and the thought of donating a kidney completely disappeared from her mind until February 1992.

She said, 'A thought or voice would come just as I was dropping off to sleep, "Now is the time to donate your kidney to Dirk". I would think to myself that I should talk to Maurice, her husband, about this but it was forgotten by the time morning came. This happened about two or three times a week for two months. I kept getting the feeling that it was perhaps God asking me to do this. I finally spoke to Maurice and he responded very positively to the idea.'

She tried to get information about my tissue type from the hospital in Groningen but there were no records any longer of my stay there. She had hoped that they would have this information so that she would be able to know whether her kidney was compatible to mine for transplantation before approaching anyone. Around this time she heard that it wasn't going well with me but this news did not compel her to proceed. A sense of duty and obligation at this point could have unhelpfully complicated things.

She decided to speak to Sandra at my parents' golden wedding anniversary when we would both be in Holland. They then decided it would be best to try to find out if her tissue type was compatible to mine. If the results proved positive they would tell me. Nevertheless Sandra was not sure I would even consider the offer.

However, this plan couldn't proceed because Wilma's doctor would not do the tests unless he had direct instructions from my doctors in England. He also informed her that it would be impossible to remove her kidney in Holland and then send it on to England for transplantation. Wilma would have preferred this because of her fear of flying.

During her stay with us we had taken Wilma to see *Les Misérables* at the Palace Theatre. The experience focused her mind on how differently she responded to the show from how Sandra and I had.

At this time she said, 'For me it was just a musical, a brilliant one perhaps, but still only a musical. I could see that you both were deeply moved by it and strongly identified with the suffering of Jean Valjean. It has been very enlightning and moving for me to be here with you this week to really see how things are with you. I now have a better understanding of what it could mean to you and the family if everything goes well in September. When you visited us in Holland we only saw you for such a short time and we were so busy with our own lives. Because of this we didn't really realise how bad things were. I'm going home with a lot better knowledge of how things really are for you.'

Later Wilma told how the time had effected her more deeply than she had dared say at the time.

'You were so depressed, so beaten down and without hope. When I got back I was overwhelmed with sadness as I saw what was happening with you and your family. Many tears were shed when I got home and I felt so powerless but I did now realise what a difference it would make to all of you if the transplant worked out right.'

Since my transplant in 1980 there had been enormous strides made in the area of transplantation. One of the most significant advances had been the discovery of an immunosuppressant drug called Cyclosporin. The amazing thing about this drug is that it is selective in its action. The antibodies that seek to destroy the kidney are suppressed whilst leaving other antibodies free to fight infections. The steroids I had used previously suppressed the whole immune system causing me to be very vulnerable to infections. This new drug has a great influence on the success rate of transplantation. Before the availability of Cyclosporin a transplant could go well but the patient might nevertheless die from an infection, not being able to fight it off.

Everything was arranged for Wilma to come back to Britain in early September for the transplant. We were counting the days. Finally on 9 September I was admitted for some final tests. Wilma, who had come over from Holland with my parents, was to come in the next day. Everyone seemed confident and in good spirits. The excitement mounted.

On the morning of 11 September we were both wheeled into the theatre from our respective wards.

As I left the dialysis unit I hoped and prayed I would never have to come back to that awful place again.

Mr Parrott came in for a final word of encouragement. Both Wilma and I appreciated the personal interest he showed in us. Next came the anaesthetist to do his work, a small prick and 'Start counting backwards from ten'. I recall the feeling of pleasant drowsiness but don't even remember getting to zero. The next thing I was aware of was slowly surfacing to consciousness in a large, unfamiliar room. A nurse suddenly appeared as she saw me opening my eyes and gently gave me the reassurance my heart had sought. Putting her hand tenderly on mine she said, 'Everything went fine, dear. Your sister is well too.' Whether it was the after-effect of the anaesthetic or just that the impossible had finally happened, I could hardly take it in. Over and over again Sandra had prayed, 'God, have mercy on us'. Even the crude language of my prayers had been answered. The prayers of our family and the prayers of so many friends had finally been answered.

I had been rescued at birth by the warmth of my mother's body. I had been saved as a child when I drank poison. I escaped death as a teenager. I was alive even after twice suffering renal failure. Cancer had been halted before it could set off on its deadly path. Maybe God has a purpose for my life after all!

Later that day Sandra phoned up the unit to hear how things were going. 'The transplant is successful, both are recovering well! In fact, Dirk has already started passing urine.' She was overwhelmed by the news, tears started streaming down her face as she walked into the lounge to tell my parents but she couldn't get her words out. My parents feared the worst, thinking that it had all gone wrong, waiting with bated breath. Finally . . . 'He's . . . he's passing urine!!' Rarely had what would have been such mundane, even impolite news create such emotion. They all hugged each other and wept for a while.

My father said he felt like Simeon, who after seeing the baby Jesus in the temple had said, 'Lord, now let your servant depart in peace . . . For my eyes have seen your salvation.' He had seen the son, for whom he had wept so many times as he worked among his plants and flowers, saved by his precious daughter.

He was also deeply moved and grateful to the people who mounted a prayer vigil at our church during the operation. 'They are praying for my son and daughter in there.' He had wanted to go in to join them but felt he wouldn't be able to cope with his own emotions.

The transplanted kidney had started working immediately. I was passing urine, the impurity levels in my blood decreased rapidly, the pains in my joints disappeared but the most dramatic change was with my mind. It was as if scales fell from my eyes and I could suddenly see clearly. The fog that had been in my head for so long suddenly lifted. A song by Hothouse Flowers, that I had listened to many times on my Walkman, rang in my mind as the tears flowed:

> I can see clearly now, the rain has gone . . .
> Gone are the dark clouds that had me blind,
> It's gonna be bright sunshiney day!
> Think I can make it now, the pain has gone,
> All the bad feelings have disappeared,
> Here is the rainbow I've been praying for,
> Look all around there's nothing but blue skies,
> Look straight ahead there's nothing but blue skies . . .

The impurities in my system had affected everything. Dialysis reduces impurity levels but not as efficiently as a transplant. Before dialysis my creatinine (a measurement of impurities) would usually be around 1300, with dialysis taking it down to 700. One day after transplantation it came down to 500 and soon afterwards normal levels were maintained.

The first person I wanted to talk to after the operation was Sandra so I asked for a phone to be brought into the room. Even before Sandra could see me she noticed a huge change, just in the tone of my voice. Before the transplant my speech had become more and more slurred with concentration becoming increasingly difficult. Now as she spoke to me she found she was speaking with the person she remembered from so many years ago. The difference overwhelmed her so much she could hardly speak! The sparkle had returned to my eyes, the certainty to my speech.

But how had things been for Wilma?

Amazingly the night before the operation she had spoken with a man who had donated a kidney to his son a week earlier. She had asked him about his experiences. He was very positive and said that seeing his son improve so dramatically had made it all very worthwhile. He also told about the pain that he experienced after coming around from the operation. She found that talking to this man and another person, who had also donated a kidney to a son, helped prepare her for what was to come.

During and after the transplant she had a strong sense of being 'upheld' by God but on the second night she had a dreadful time. A system had been recently introduced that allows the patients to regulate their own intake of pain killer by pressing a button which releases small amounts of morphine into the blood stream. Wilma's system had not been properly connected so no amount of pressing on the button brought relief. Enquiries for the staff to do something about the pain were not properly attended to. When the nurse found her weeping they finally realised that something was wrong. The equipment was checked and the fault corrected. I, too, had some difficulties in understanding the system and was confused as to how it worked. Both of us found it difficult to absorb procedural information after coming round from the operation and were surprised that they just left us to it.

Wilma enjoyed the informality in the relationships with doctors and consultants. In Holland you did not address any senior doctor by his first name, never mind the senior consultant! The sense of togetherness she found in the ward with the other patients was very special to her.

In fact, she found it so distressing to observe a nurse being uncaring and very off-hand with an elderly patient that she felt she had to speak to someone about the situation. 'It could have been our mother,' she said to me.

The attention she received from my friends she found to be very special and was overwhelmed by the kindness she received. She wasn't expecting it. She enjoyed all the beautiful flowers, cards and gifts, often from people she didn't even know.

She said she was thankful that God was willing to use her. Thankful that everything came together so wonderfully and had a strong sense that it was meant to be!

'Time to get you out of bed,' the nurse said to me a day or so after the transplant.

'Are you kidding, I've got all kinds of tubes coming in and out of my body?'

'No, it will help the healing process, even if you only get out for a few minutes,' came the very determined reply.

Actually, it was fine the first time but the next time the rickety old chair collapsed under me. (I'm not *that* heavy!) I frantically pressed the alarm button fearing one of the fluid lines would become disconnected. All in a day's work for the nurses though, and it even brought a little light relief to their work! 'Come and see Dirk!' they called. NHS funding didn't allow for non-essential items like firm chairs for the patients!

I was producing good quantities of urine (it may not mean a lot to you but it did to me) and steady progress was being maintained so the doctors concluded that it was the right time to remove the catheter from my bladder. The kidney was working but what about my bladder that hadn't been used in four years? At first, some urine came through but soon the flow stopped. The kidney was doing its filtering job but the container into which it fed was not releasing the fluid. The pain grew as the pressure increased in the bladder. The catheter caused spasms which were excruciatingly painful. The euphoria of the successful transplant was considerably dampened down by this new problem. The nurse, Gill, tried to reassure me that everything would be fine. 'Many patients experience difficulties with their bladders. Time is needed for it to get used to working again after not functioning for so many years.'

It was all too much for me! 'I just can't cope with it any more. I used to be able to take things, but not anymore,' I sobbed. 'You just let it out,' Gill said, putting her arm comfortingly around my shoulder. I cried for a long time, probably as much for what I felt in the past as for what I was feeling now. The doctors decided to catheterise me again for the time being.

One week after the operation Wilma came out of hospital to return home to her husband and four children but not before one final visit to M&S with Sandra. Wilma had 'lost a kidney, but gained a friend'. Partially through the increased contact the transplant gave, Sandra and Wilma grew very close. She became the sister that Sandra never had.

Wilma had been weakened by the operation and it would take her time to recover. The doctors confirmed to her that it would take some months to fully recover but that the one kidney would soon do the work previously done by the two.

Her family too, had made a huge sacrifice in having wife and mother so far away in such a dramatic and possibly dangerous situation. When Wilma came over for the operation she brought over a lovely note written by her husband, Maurice:

> Tomorrow will be the day! Even though we cannot be there with you and Wilma, we will be strongly united with you in our thoughts and prayers. We all wish you much strength and faith in 'Our Father' who so much wants to heal. We are thankful that Wilma can do this for you and that you are willing to receive this help. We look forward to the moment that you will be free from the burden and pressure of dialysis and can move towards living a more humane life.
>
> Signed with love from, Maurice, Naomi, Mattijs, Rachael, Miriam

Being so emotionally involved but having no proper outlet for his feelings Maurice had shaped a kidney out of clay. 'It helped me to work the soft material into the smooth, rounded shape.'

I had to stay in a week longer than Wilma but the waiting was made very bearable by the lovely food Sandra was bringing in from the ladies at Emmanuel-St. James church. They had organised a rota so that

The Second Transplant (1992)

Sandra and the family would have a home-cooked meal every day while I was in hospital. Sandra would also bring in some lovely treats from Marks & Spencer's. She brought in foods that would have been forbidden before, like Pecan Surprise dessert, soft dried dates and apricots and apple and mango fruit drink.

There were many cards, flowers and fruit brought to the hospital making my room look very cheerful indeed. When I got home there were even more gifts. Friends and neighbours welcomed me back. I was touched deeply by their kindness. Good neighbour Pam said, 'You look leaner and fitter'.

I felt like a new person, wanting to change to be a new and better person. There was so much I wanted to do, so much food I wanted to stuff myself with! Mandy observed, 'There is a lot more laughter in this house than there used to be'. Stephen said, 'The only way I can describe it is that it feels like Christmas!'

When Christmas came it was very different. I could have a mince pie when I felt like it. I could eat Sandra's beautiful, exotic, fruit-filled Christmas cake with my coffee, not saving it until I was on the machine. I could have a glass of beer or wine when I felt like it.

I felt as if I had been released from prison or, more appropriately, raised from the dead! The pallor of my skin improved, more ruddy now. Gone was the 'putty' look. My hair grew thicker and my eyebrows were bushier, though that was one of the unusual side effects of Cyclosporin.

One day I was walking down the street and greeted the father of a friend of mine but he didn't respond. Suddenly he spun around in his tracks, 'It's you! I didn't recognise you.' That happened more than once!

My bladder however, was still giving me trouble. After some weeks at home I went back into hospital to have the catheter removed. I passed urine normally, if painfully, for a few days but gradually it was reduced to a trickle and then stopped altogether. I was devastated and in severe pain because of the increasing pressure in my bladder. I begged the young nurse to do something, to get a doctor to come to see me. It was late at night so there was no doctor on the ward and she wasn't able to get anyone from another ward. In emergencies a senior registrar or consultant can be called out but I guess she didn't consider it urgent enough. I was so angry and frustrated, spending most of my time on a commode trying to press out a few drops of urine. Sometimes I would try to sleep but the pain was too intrusive. A bath didn't help either. I had never experienced pain like this and was especially angry at God. 'So, "all things work together for good", do they? What is this for? What possible good can come out of this? Is this to teach me something? Is this for someone else's benefit?'

'I'll show him,' I thought defiantly, 'If God treats me like this I'll watch a film he wouldn't approve of.' Conveniently there was a sleazy (Dutch!) film on that night. It was a lousy film which didn't make me feel any better and I soon regretted my foolish stance.

I continued the night in severe pain and in the morning a junior doctor came to take a blood test. He was not very experienced and would often have to have a few 'goes' before he found a suitable vein. No way was he going to take my blood! I felt a bit sorry for him because it wasn't his fault that my veins were sometimes difficult to locate. If he found no blood supply in my arm he would try the back of my hand which looked easier but wasn't.

Finally the doctors did their rounds but I was at the end of the ward so I was the last to be seen. It was decided to catheterise me again. The doctors also decided that I should see the consultant Urologist Dr Payne (that is his real name) to consider what should be done next.

'I think the only solution is to make a small incision in the neck of the bladder,' he said. This had been done before with good results, though there is 50% chance of you losing the ability to ejaculate. That concentrated my mind wonderfully! Was I willing to risk losing sexual pleasure to gain good bladder function? I didn't have much choice really. I couldn't live without a proper bladder function.

The operation was done and I was soon passing urine again normally. (I was able to regain some sexual function but it was never the same again.) There was one significant difference between this time and the last in that I was able to hold a lot more urine in my bladder. In the eighties my sleep was always broken by the need for three or four visits to the toilet. Now as a result of my bladder being stretched on that fateful night I was able to sleep the night through. I found it ironic that just when I decided to throw down the gauntlet God brought good out of the pain I was experiencing. Even though it took a few months before I could pass urine without pain it certainly felt good to be able to urinate normally again. How I used to envy the men who could just walk up to the urinal, relieve themselves, zip up and walk away without giving it a moment's thought! What had taken me six hours three times a week they could do painlessly, whenever they felt like it. Now I was able to join their ranks.

17

New Horizons (1994–98)

'A Positive Life'
Stefan Pierlejewski

One of the things we were so much looking forward to was the chance to get away for a while. I was still under intensive control by the hospital so going abroad was out of the question but we were allowed to have a break in Britain. We booked a pretty little cottage in Week St. Mary in Cornwall. It is the sort of village where you expected to come across Miss Marple at any moment.

Cornwall has so many pretty seaside villages, lovely beaches and hidden coves to explore. After one of these days touring we returned to our peaceful little cottage to find our way blocked by the police! Our cottage had been cordoned off. There were police cars, fire engines and ambulances around our house. The press was there and apparently a psychiatrist too. We weren't allowed in because three children were being kept hostage next door and the hostage taker was ready to set off a bomb if anyone approached. He had hung a huge banner out of the top-floor window reading 'CANADIAN JUSTICE??' crudely written with a paintbrush. We heard from the residents that he was a man with a violent past who wasn't being allowed access into Canada to see his children so he had taken some Canadian children hostage whilst they were on holiday in Britain.

We had arrived at the opposite end of the village to where our cottage was. After many hours of waiting we were told we would be put up in the village hotel at the expense of the Cornwall Police department. We were not allowed to drive through the village to get to the other side because that took us past our house so we had to go around on country roads to get to the hotel. We got completely lost travelling up and down the high-banked country roads in pitch darkness. A journey that could have taken a few minutes took an hour. We arrived back in the village feeling very tense.

Before we did this, there was another problem however. The Cyclosporin tablets were in the house along with my sermon notes for a wedding the next day! We mentioned this to the police who reluctantly offered one of the military-style, Special Squad to go in to get the things I needed. I explained to them where the tablets and the notes were, or at least where I hoped they would be. At last someone recognised the value of my sermon notes! They were duly retrieved and we drove off to our hotel to sleep. It took us some time to wake the landlord who was a

New Horizons (1994–98)

little reluctant to believe our story. It was a very luxurious hotel and Sandra and I were given the bridal suite. We hardly slept a wink and I can assure you it was not for the usual reason 'newly-weds' don't sleep!

The next morning we went to see how things were going and were amazed to see that it was all over. The children were safe and the father had no bomb and had given himself up. We were so glad that it had all ended peacefully. Just being in the proximity of where there might be violence done to children had left us feeling very frightened and uneasy. We were aware that it could have ended so differently.

We needed a holiday to recover from our holiday so later in the year we booked a pretty cottage in Salisbury. This time we had a lovely relaxing time.

We walked along the old-fashioned streets, we shopped among the Christmas decorations, we ate all the foods in abundance that I wasn't previously allowed. I ate the most enormous piece of chocolate cake. We discovered and were deeply moved by Delibes, *The Flower Duet* and listened to Classic FM for the first time. We visited the cathedral, joining in at evensong. Thompy and Gill visited, with whom we talked deeply as they too were recovering from the effects of Gill's recent serious illness.

Another friend who called was Rob Wood, who wanted to interview us for the Navigators news-sheet. Talking to him gave me an opportunity to give focus to some of my thoughts.

'There is a lot of meaningless suffering in the world and I think that is something we Christians find hard to stomach!' I said in response to a question regarding what I had learned about suffering in the last four years. 'I do not always see a golden purpose in everything. I am sure that there is one in the broad sense but when you pin it down to a particular set of circumstances it is often extremely hard to see God at work. Suffering is part of being human and Christians are not immune to it. What you are left with is a huge mystery.'

I told him that the experience of the last four years made me uneasy with the sort of theology which says suffering always equals a sense of closeness to God and is therefore a reason to be joyful.

I had received letters saying, 'You must be learning a lot and experiencing God in a special way.' What I found so difficult about the recent past was that I did not experience the closeness of God. Because of the persistent pain I could never really concentrate. I felt as if there was a sort of fog over my eyes when I tried to read the Bible. It was very frustrating for me not to be able to remember what I had been reading a few minutes earlier.

I was too close to the recent events to come up with any conclusions but one thing that had impressed me from the book of Lamentations was that God brought darkness into Jeremiah's life A 24-hour day has within it both day and night, light and darkness. I accept darkness as part of my day and possibly there is a parallel here with the Christian life. If God wants me to live in darkness for a time there is not a lot I can do about it even if I hate it. The danger I faced was to lose my faith in the darkness, and to become angry with God.

Rob asked me whether I had done either of those.

I replied, 'Most of the time I felt like a beaten dog and I did not have the strength to fight even if I wanted to. I don't think I lost my faith but I sometimes entered into what I would call "faith's no-man's land". I stopped expecting a solution and didn't really think about things at all! I would adopt a passive acceptance of things rather than actively believing that God's will would be fulfilled for his glory. Sandra used to say that it is like being in prison, and that is often how I felt.'

The first year of our new life was spent enjoying our new life together. I had a minimal involvement with work realising that I had a long way to go to recover emotionally and spiritually. The physical improvement had been so significant but there were still some side effects of the drugs that needed to be seen to.

We had a strong sense of new horizons opening up for us. I remember so well having a sense of death being on the horizon. What a different perspective there was now.

First of all we felt we needed learn to walk closer with God. We had been struck by a definition of sin we heard from Lawrence Crabb: 'believing that God is not good enough to be trusted'. We felt that the experiences of the last few years had eroded our confidence in God and even weakened us spiritually. We had experienced so many disappointments that we were now quite surprised if things went well!

Since 'faith comes by hearing,' we spent time seeking God in the scriptures and other writings. The books of Henri Nouwen, a Dutch priest and scholar, proved very helpful to us because he expressed a 'vulnerable' Christianity we could relate to. (Henri Nouwen reaches the parts other writers cannot reach!) I also reread some of the classics I had read in my youth like *The Imitation of Christ* by Thomas à Kempis and Bunyan's *Pilgrim's Progress* to rediscover my early enthusiasm for God.

Secondly we felt that we needed to develop a new lifestyle. We sensed that God had given us a new gift of life and freedom that we didn't have before. We both found a marked reluctance to let circumstances or duty determine what we did. We wanted to respond eagerly to life's opportunities but not out of a sense of obligation. I suppose that having been forced by circumstances to live in a particular way we didn't want to create a new bondage for ourselves.

I asked myself, 'What is life about anyway?' The writer of Ecclesiastes wrestled with this question too. He seemed to say that achievements as such are not what life is about; it's more about making the best of the process. i.e. enjoying the ordinary things like our relationships, our work, our possessions and ultimately to relate well to God and do what he says. I noticed that when I went about my hobby gardening I did it with such intensity that the pleasure went out of it. It became accomplishing a goal rather than enjoying a process.

We wanted to enjoy our daughter, sons and grandson. We wanted to enjoy our work whether it was Sandra's colour consulting or our involvement with people. Shopping didn't have to be a chore. I could even learn to enjoy pushing the trolley around the supermarket!

We also felt that there might be some new horizons opening up in our service of God. How did God want to use us in the next few years, we asked ourselves. Someone said that one's gifts are like capital and our experience like the interest on the capital. How should these be invested now to maximum benefit?

I was impressed by a painful experience the prophet Hosea had. God said that he was to marry an unfaithful woman. He was to continue loving her and being faithful to her even if she wasn't true to him. This was meant to be a sign that God would continue to love Israel even when she was unfaithful. Hosea was meant to be a visual aid, a living message showing God's faithful love.

I asked myself, 'What does God want to say through our lives?' I didn't believe it was for us to say but we heard from others that they took encouragement from our lives to carry on. Others saw our love and acceptance of our children as showing God's faithfulness and patience. I would not have chosen this set of circumstances but my desire for many years had been that people would be helped to see God through our lives.

The work to hand was to serve and counsel the Navigator staff in the northern part of Britain, about ten in all. We were looking forward to having more meaningful involvement after being on the edge of things for so many years.

We also wanted to strengthen our involvement with our ever-changing family.

Mandy had recently started teaching infants in a local primary school and was loving it. She seemed so well suited to the task. What a blessing and relief it was to see her finally able to do the work she had been preparing for for so long. She shared a flat with four others not far from us.

Mark's future was somewhat obscure at the time. He had trained as a bricklayer, but had no real opportunity to develop this. He worked in the building trade periodically. Though he didn't see a long-term future there he wasn't clear about an alternative either. We were grateful that his diabetes was well managed giving him few side effects. The great joy in his life was Kyle and he loved spending time with 'Little V'. (Mark is called 'Vany' by his friends.) Kyle commented at the time, 'My dad makes me laugh and I make him laugh!'

Stephen had recently passed his driving test and took every opportunity he could to drive our car. He was going into the second year of his 'A' levels and was thinking about doing further studies in Business at University. He was actually more interested in creating music on his computer!

Throughout the years of dialysis we were often reminded of our need for friends. We noticed particularly that as the days darkened for us it had the

New Horizons (1994–98)

effect of moving us away from people. At the time Sandra had observed, 'illness isolates'. There was less time and emotional energy available for other people. We now felt that we were in a stronger position to reconnect with neglected friends. One thing that surprised us was that there had actually been changes in our relationships with some people during the time of ill health. Those who had been able to support and show compassion had come closer. This had especially happened in our relationship with James and Jan Broad. Over the past few years Sandra and Jan had spent hours on the phone. It was a real lifeline for Sandra. The relationship with those who 'didn't know what to do', and had therefore done little, had lessened. We wanted to seek to restore and build where we could.

Our friends were often not local so we realised we would need to travel and phone to keep in touch and thankfully we were now in a position to do this.

Not only were we able to travel but we were also able to have people come to us to celebrate the new life. Within an eight-month period we had opportunities for three very special celebrations. Mandy was married to Stefan Pierlejewski on 22 October 1994. The following January we celebrated my fiftieth birthday and on 7 June our twenty-fifth wedding anniversary. Each was special in its own right but the fact that we never really expected me to be alive for any of them added so much joy and gratitude.

Mandy and Stefan's wedding was an incredible mixture of the old and new. A classic Morgan sports car took the modern-looking bride to church. (The father of the bride looked pretty modern too for an old 'fella'.) Modern music, (created by Stefan, a musician) rang through the 17th-century church. The traditional C. of E. wedding service was interrupted by loud cheering when the vicar John Mills pronounced them 'man and wife'. The formal service was interspersed with creative prayers. Even the vicar went down very well with the crowd in his rainbow scarf!

The reception carried on the theme of mixing old and new. Traditional wedding party food was served to informal seating arrangements – no top table. The bride's father's speech was a musical 'This is Your Life', starting off with a surprise recording of Mandy singing at age two, followed by songs of her childhood and on into the teenage years. It was a very mixed company. It doesn't happen very often that Beethoven, Abba, Led Zeppelin and Barry Manilow, singing 'Mandy' ('You came and you gave without taking'), appear on the same programme together. The honour of the final tune came from Stefan's own recently released CD of 'ambient' music, *A Positive Life*.

Finally the wedding cake was served. It looked the same as any other until closer inspection revealed 'love heart' sweets around the surface of the cake. Not a fruit cake mix on the inside either!

The next big day was my birthday. There was no energy left for a big do so we just had an intimate celebration together as a family. Anyway we could look forward to something special on 7 June.

New Horizons (1994–98)

We felt we wanted to have our friends, family and neighbours around us in our home. In fact, one of our neighbours had her own catering business so we could commit all the cooking to her. And what a spread was provided. A whole poached salmon, pieces of chicken, savoury roulade (especially for vegetarians but they were lucky to get a piece). There was a variety of salads, cheeses, breads and relishes. It was all very delicious and we had sufficient but were unable to resist the lovely desserts of sherry trifle, pavlova, lemon mousse, fresh fruit and even a special '25'-shaped cake. We received some lovely presents too, some made out of silver. We used one of the gifts to drink champagne out of!

We listened to a recording of some of our wedding service. I found the loud, brash speech given by the young Canadian bridegroom rather irritating. I think he has mellowed over the years. We even had an old colour cine-film of our wedding put onto video cassette to watch, complete with cringe-making background music, 'The Bells are Ringing' and 'Making Woopee'. Lots of laughs and comments about the sixties-style clothing! The culmination of the evening was a short but touching word Mandy gave on behalf of our three grown-up children.

In the Autumn of 1994 the Dutch Navigators invited me to go to Holland to participate in a conference that was going to look at the issue of suffering, specifically focusing on the question of why God allows it. Though reluctant to get involved in this issue I realised that this was perhaps the opportunity

I needed to try to give focus to my own thoughts and feelings. I was finding my way back to God but I was still hurting about the past and confused at times too. The maxim that, 'God was too wise to make mistakes and too loving to be unkind' wasn't helping anymore. I think this was because so many 'mistakes' and too many 'unkind' things had happened to me. My feelings would often be brought to the surface if I felt someone was minimising or glorifying suffering in some way.

I remember vividly that on television a priest, when being interviewed about suffering, had replied that 'suffering is good for you'. I had very strong reactions to tragedies being presented as something out of which good comes automatically thereby ignoring the pain and tragedy.

I remember an account in a Christian publication giving glorious reports of how the church in South Africa, that had suffered a violent attack, many being killed, was now growing and flourishing as a result. I didn't doubt the truth of this report but I thought 'Tell that to the child who lost her parents on the sacrificial altar of "Benefit to Others".'

I realised that I needed some answers to these questions. I started my project by reading some books on the subject of suffering. I felt that most of the books were what I would call 'looking on the bright side', which always put me in mind of the Monty Python song that Eric Idle sang in *The Life of Brian*. A spoof song sung at the hero's death. 'Always look on the bright side of life, te dum, te dum . . .'

New Horizons (1994–98)

One book I read seemed to suggest that if your 'theology of suffering' was right everything would be fine. Another put forward the case that you may feel useless but God is using your life for display purposes i.e. to show his glory. Another felt that no price was too great to pay for the privilege of witnessing to Christ because the world takes notice of those who have severe handicaps. One of the most pathetic attempts to help was putting forward the thesis that pain is a gift from God to protect us from dangers i.e. a fire burns thereby warning you to keep away.

I believe C.S. Lewis was enthusiastic about the idea that pain is God's megaphone, as he wrote in *The Problem of Pain*. When his wife died there was no trace of this helping him through the despair he experienced that he so eloquently recorded in *A Grief Observed*.

Now I have to say that I felt each writer had a very valid point but they didn't help me. It was as if each one added to my pain by making it seem illegitimate.

One exceptional book that I read in the seventies, *A Step Further* by Joni Eareckson and Steve Estes, and reread, was as good as I had remembered it the first time. The chapter entitled 'Let God be God', which addresses the mystery and sovereignty of God, drawing especially on the book of Job, is outstanding. The other book I appreciate very much is *The Wounded Healer*, by Henri Nouwen, published in the same year. The key thought that I have taken from this book is: 'Who can take away suffering without entering it?' This applies foremost to Jesus but also to anyone who wants to bring healing.

The first question I sought to address was, 'How does God feel about all the suffering in the world?' As I was mulling over this question I was suddenly reminded of the fact that if I want to know what God thinks about something, Jesus is the person I should address. In the Bible, he is called 'the visible expression of the invisible God'. He came for the express purpose of making God's ways known. From my study there were three main thoughts that stood out to me.

The first thing I noticed was how Jesus continually expressed a heart of deep love and compassion for the people he met. This drew my attention to how he demonstrates his love for me by his emotional involvement with me. He weeps when I weep, he feels my pain. I used to think that Jesus' suffering didn't last as long as mine until I realised that he was and still is suffering because of what is happening to people like me. He showed how much he cared for Lazarus by weeping at his graveside. Those who saw his tears observed, 'See how he loved him!' The fact that he was about to raise Lazarus from the dead didn't block his emotional involvement. I could imagine a modern Christian saying to Jesus, 'You shouldn't be crying, you should be celebrating his life or at least rejoicing at the imminent reappearance of your friend!' Jesus was able to cope with other people's pain and enter into it.

The next thought that stood out to me was that he loved me so much and cared about my pain so much that he died on the cross to make the way possible for me to come to God to be restored and forgiven.

I think for the sufferer (at least this was how I felt) the only thing desired is to be relieved of the pain, to be rescued, to be freed. Having someone explain that there is a good purpose to all things didn't help me very much. Perhaps it helped at first but not when the pain intensified or seemed to go on forever. The circumstances said, 'You are not loved!' The basic feeling I had was one of being unloved, not a person of any value. When someone came along and gave reassurance of being loved and valued I was helped.

I found so often that people didn't know what to say, perhaps not realising that I didn't need a word so much as an expression of love.

The greatest and most significant statement about my being loved and valuable comes from Jesus. I believe Jesus' death on the cross is the fundamental 'answer to my suffering'. He has proven his love for me by giving up everything that was dear to him. *'Greater love has no man than that he lay down his life for his friends.'*

What perhaps surprised me most in my study was the thought that Jesus did what he could by healing, feeding, teaching and even raising from the dead, but that he didn't do this universally or even for all the people in Israel who had needs, for that matter. He raised Lazarus from the dead but allowed the much-loved John the Baptist to die a horrible death. This touches for me on the mystery of God and his ways. I understand something, i.e. God loves me, but I don't understand why he heals some and not others. Why didn't he feed the world with his loaves and fishes rather than just the five thousand? He raised Lazarus from the dead but didn't the next time he died. Nor did he raise John the Baptist who was 'the greatest in the kingdom'. I concluded from this truth that there is much that happens in our lives we simply cannot understand. I find I cannot relate to people who see God's hand in everything that happens in their lives, good or bad. It seems to me that there are too many complex factors at work in life.

Some things that happen to me are a result of my wrongdoing, other things by someone else's wrongdoing. Satan also has a major role in what happens on earth, a place where he has very great power. Sometimes God grants what we ask, at other times not.

God mightily led the Israelites across the Red Sea but at other times they had to use a boat! The Bible is full of God's mighty acts, but to quote Eric Liddell in *Chariots of Fire*, 'I don't believe the Almighty orders his day around me'.

What do I conclude from the different ways God acts? Humbly to accept my circumstances but not to claim to understand everything that happens and give it a divine purpose.

I had questions that I was looking for answers to, but also feelings I was seeking to learn to live with.

I still feel very emotionally vulnerable. Sensitivity towards my own pain seems to have made me feel more acutely the pain of others. Certain TV programmes, especially true to life ones, I have to avoid. Television presents us with powerful images about which we are often quite powerless to do anything. Even certain fiction like *Casualty* I won't watch because it stimulates too much emotion that I can't handle. Music too can touch me very deeply. I'll never forget seeing The Royal Opera House production of Verdi's *La Traviata* with Angela Gheorghiu. I cried from beginning to end and it wasn't just at the sad story. I was crying mostly to express my own pain.

Another feeling I had was that God owes me a pleasant and trouble-free life from here on, after allowing so much trouble to come my way. This feeling was perhaps stimulated by what I read about Job: 'The Lord made him prosperous again and gave him twice as much as he had before. The Lord blessed the later part of Job's life more than the first.'

I felt that I had had my share of difficulty in this life so I was very wary of getting involved with people and situations that would cause me pain. I sensed God encouraging me to get involved even if it was going to be difficult. 'Who can take away suffering without entering it?' In fact, things turned out to be more difficult than I had ever imagined. In the first place, I felt weaker and more vulnerable than in the past, but the circumstances also led to some alienation from friends and this hurt me very deeply. Perhaps because of growing up as a self-sufficient young man in Canada I always had the idea that I didn't care what people thought of me. How wrong I was! I wanted to be liked and appreciated.

The depth of my feelings really came home to me one day as I was driving along the M6 coming down from a visit to Scotland. I was reflecting on some of the difficulties I was experiencing then and in the past. Suddenly tears welled up in my eyes. 'I want to be appreciated.' I wept to myself for a while hardly being able to see where I was going. The tears proved to my heart the strength of my feelings about this matter. To be honest I was a little surprised at the strength of them.

Over the years it seems as if not only the route from my eyes to my heart has shortened but also my heart to my eyes. I am easily moved by what I see and tears come readily.

I feel as if the experiences of my life and especially the last five or ten years have left me with an open wound that I feel most acutely in my relationship to God. Some hymns and Christian songs I can hardly bear to sing. One of the best/worst is:

> Faithful one, so unchanging . . .
> I call out to you again and again,
> You are my rock in times of trouble,
> You lift me up when I fall down.
> All through the storm your love is the anchor . . .
>
> (Brian Doerkson)

(I'm already crying as I write this!)

It is usually the line, 'I call out to you again and again' that first moves me deeply. In my mind I see myself on the kidney machine. I am reconnected with the pain of those circumstances and my desperate pleas to God to save me. I felt it took him so long to come to my aid.

New Horizons (1994–98)

But the line, 'All through the storm your love is the answer' puts me in touch with my deepest feelings about God. His love is the answer and I love him. I probably love him more now than I did or perhaps I am only more aware of how I feel about him. Whichever it is, I feel more closely connected to him.

I am a new man, like one resurrected from the dead. I feel better now than I have done since my youth. Age has taken its toll but my spirit has been renewed. I am enjoying my new work of mentoring leaders in the wider context of the Navigators in Britain and speaking at various gatherings.

Sandra continues to bring 'colour' into people's lives wherever she goes. Wilma too, who saved my life, is keeping well.

I am grateful . . .

Organ Donation

'Dutch Courage' demonstrates clearly the extent to which a successful transplant can improve the quality of life not only of the patient concerned, but also of close family members. Latest available information* shows that, whilst the number of people waiting for a kidney transplant is growing, the number of such operations being carried out has plateaued.

Saving the life of any patient is always the paramount concern of hospital staff, but, sadly, some patient will not recover. It is only after a series of medical tests have been carried out by senior doctors who have no connection at all with transplantation that the question of possible organ donation will be raised.

No organs will be removed if those close to the patient do not wish donation to take place. However, it is much easier for hospital staff to raise the matter with families if they know that the patient had expressed a wish to donate, and this can be checked before approaching the family by reference to the National Organ Donor Register database held at the United Kingdom Transplant Support Services Authority in Bristol.

Similarly, at a time of tremendous personal grief for the patient's family, it is easier for them to come to a decision to agree to donation if they have discussed the subject within the family previously, and

---

*Source UKTSSA Transplant Activity Report 1997

are aware of the patient's own wishes on the subject. Indeed, many families say that they derive some comfort at such an emotional time from the knowledge that they have respected the wishes of their loved one and, in so doing, have brought new hope to other families, as a result of donation.

The gift of life is a precious one which cannot be bought, but is the ultimate expression of selfless love from one human being to another.

Organ donor register forms, which contain an organ donor card, can be obtained from a number of sources such as G.P.s surgeries, pharmacies, and health related charities. They can also be obtained by phoning 0845 6060400.

Dennis Crane
National Kidney Federation Representative

On Asking God Why?
trusting God in a twisted world
Elisabeth Elliot

"I seek the lessons God wants to teach me, and that means that I ask why."

In this collection of meditations well-loved author Elisabeth Elliot addresses many of the difficult questions and issues that we face in our lives. With great insight and candour she explores subjects ranging from abortion and divorce to tenderness and birthdays.

Throughout *On Asking God Why* readers are encouraged to question their Father and allow themselves to trust Him without reservation, because in Him every answer is found.

Elisabeth Elliot has written numerous books including *Keep a Quiet Heart* and *A Path Through Suffering*. She is a popular speaker and, at present, hosts a radio programme in the USA called "Gateway to Joy".

ISBN 1-85078-276-8

OM publishing

Answer to Tough Questions
About the Christian Faith
Josh McDowell & Don Stewart

- How can we believe a Bible full of contradictions?
- Why is Jesus the only way to God?
- Don't all religions basically teach the same thing?
- If Christianity is so great, why are there so few Christians?

Josh McDowell and Don Stewart answer these and dozens more questions.

Over 50 questions are covered, dealing with a wide range of subjects including God, the Person of Christ, miracles, the Bible and what it really means to be a Christian.

Josh McDowell, a graduate of Wheaton College and Talbot Theological Seminary, is a travelling speaker for Campus Crusade for Christ. During the last 20 years he has spoken in over 60 countries to more than seven million young people and adults. He is also author of several bestselling books, including *Evidence That Demands a Verdict* Volumes 1 and 2, *The Father Connection* and co-author with Don Stewart of *Reasons Why We Should Consider Christianity*.

ISBN 0-94651-551-4

alpha

Judy: A Second Chance
She Refused to Give Up
Judy Mbugua

Married at eighteen against her parents' wishes, Judy thought she could thrive exclusively on love. Soon she had to face the realities: her parents disapproved of her marriage, she had children to feed and clothe, bills to pay against a small income, she was jobless with little education and no skills. Her husband still loved her but she was miserable and lost. Was she being punished for her mistakes? In tears and distress, she began to search for answers. When all seemed lost and hopeless, God intervened and gave her a second chance.

Today, Judy is among the few renowned and respected women personalities in international Christian leadership circles. A speaker evangelist and teacher, her responsiblities include the international chairperson of AD 2000 Women Track, and the Continental Co-ordinator for the Pan African Christian Women Alliance.

Judy: A Second Chance offers hope to all who are in despair after seeing failures and puts forward the challenge to never give up – our God is the God of second chances.

"Headstrong and rebellious, she defiles her family's cultural standard and Christian teaching. But God saw the potential in this capable young African woman. He gave her a second chance to make her a powerful tool for the gospel across the continent and the world. This book will convince every reader

that God is willing to give a second chance to anyone who comes to Him in repentance and obedience."
Lorry Lutz, International Co-ordinator, AD 2000 Women's Track

"What a privilege and blessing it has been to know Judy Mbugua. She has been a voice for African women from whom we seldom hear."
George Verwer, International Director, Operation Mobilisation

ISBN 1-85078-337-3

OM publishing